Julia Kristina, MA Psych. is a master therapist and mindset coach who helps smart, empathic people get past anxiety, stress, and self-doubt so they can have better, live better, and feel better.

Through her online membership program, The Shift Society, she helps heart centred humans identify the thoughts and beliefs that are holding them back, and then teaches them how to take charge of their thoughts and emotions so they can thrive in all areas of their lives.

Julia's expertise has been featured in Inc magazine, Psych Central, Mind Body Green and numerous other publications, podcasts and television outlets. She has also given talks in front of audiences of hundreds on stages across North America. Videos on her YouTube channel have been watched more than 14 million times and she has built a community of over 325,000 fans across social media platforms. When she's not helping her clients and students increase their emotional intelligence and build their mental resilience, she's either reading another psychology book, having a dance party in her kitchen, or on some kind of outdoor adventure with her three small children in Vancouver BC, Canada.

DRIVE YOUR OWN DARN BUS!

HOW TO GET MENTALLY STRONG

AND INTO THE DRIVER'S SEAT

OF YOUR OWN LIFE

JULIA KRISTINA

WATKINS

Sharing Wisdom Since 1893

Drive Your Own Darn Bus
Julia Kristina

First published in the UK and USA 2022 by
Watkins, an imprint of Watkins Media Limited
Unit 11, Shepperton House
89–93 Shepperton Road
London N1 3DF

enquiries@watkinspublishing.com

A CIP record for this book is available from the British Library
ISBN: 978-1-78678-472-8

1 2 3 4 5 6 7 8 9 10

Set in Adobe Garamond Pro
Printed in the United Kingdom by TJ Books

www.watkinspublishing.com

CONTENTS

INTRODUCTION

I spend most of my days dealing with other people's struggles. They come to me saying things like, "I need to stop getting stuck in paralyzing self-doubt whenever I'm about to step into something new" or, "I want to stop obsessing about everything that comes out of my mouth and worrying about whether someone took what I said the wrong way" or, "I want to lie in bed at night without stressing about all the people who rely on me, and everything I need to get done for them so they don't get upset" or, "I need my thoughts to stop spinning out of control and getting anxious about everything terrible that could happen!" I listen with intent, help people reshape their relationship with these struggles, and work with them to find solutions they can put into action. Seems like I'm a great friend, huh? I mean, I am, but dealing with issues like these is all in a day's work for me—I'm a therapist with a thriving practice and the founder of *The Shift Society*, an online community where people learn how to take charge of their thoughts and emotions and live authentically by doing the hard, intentional work of healing, growing, and shifting.

Over time, I've come to realize that struggles like these have the power to dominate our lives, or at least distract us from the things that are most important to us. The energy it takes to deal with these issues leeches our ability to live fully, love as freely as we can, and ultimately have the courage to create the life we want most. These common struggles determine how we feel, the health of our relationships, and how we perform at our jobs every single day. We think (mistakenly) that if [insert problem here] was solved, life would be easy and we could finally find happiness.

Well, friend, I've got good news and bad news.

Let's get the bad news over with first. The bad news is that solving a singular problem in your life is not the secret to peace, nor is it the key to happiness. After all, you've done it before, haven't you? You've finally gotten your boss to back off, your partner to start pitching in more, you've met the goal, fulfilled everyone else's needs, and you've even ticked everything off your to-do list, but your happiness stocks didn't really rise all that much, did they? I hate to say it, but this pattern, if unchecked, will continue for a lifetime. You might work extra hard to control everything in your environment, be on top of it all, get promoted quickly, win the approval of your parents, or the validation of everyone around you. But even if you achieve all those things, the same underlying stressors will inevitably pop up again. I know, it's hard to hear, but stay with me. The good news comes next.

Just because achieving your goals, changing your circumstances, or gaining approval won't solve all your problems, it doesn't mean your problems are permanent, or that something is fundamentally wrong with you. I, too, struggled with falling into the same rut for years. I thought there was some secret to happiness that I could obtain by changing the people around me, achieving all of my goals, avoiding anything challenging, or becoming anyone other than myself. I struggled with anxiety, was full of self-doubt, and felt like I'd missed the day in school when I was supposed to be taught how to be a regular human. But I couldn't seem to help the fact that I was stuck in a never-ending cycle:

- I'd work really hard—like *really* hard—but never felt as though what I was doing was good enough, or even like *I* was good enough.

- I'd stress about things—mainly things I could do nothing about—but I just couldn't stop the overthinking and incessant worry.
- I'd try to do what I thought people wanted of me, so that I'd "fit in" and they'd like me.
- I'd perpetually second-guess my decisions and, no matter the stakes, inevitably stressed that I made the wrong one.
- I'd feel like an outsider and take most things personally, including—you're going to laugh when I say this—dogs barking at me. That's right. I would be walking past a dog and if it suddenly started barking at me, I'd worry I'd done something to deserve it. As a therapist who helps others overcome anxiety and self-doubt, yes, I see the irony.

But then, one life-changing day, I found something called "thought work": the concept that, more often than not, it's **not** the situation, person, or conversation that's causing your intense emotional reaction; it's your thoughts, beliefs, ideas, and your perception about whatever is happening (or not happening) that sends you into an emotional tailspin.

Take a minute to let that sink in. It's not what's happening, it's how you *interpret* what's happening that causes the freefall.

When I learned about this concept, I was blown away. I dug deep and realized I was constantly running every experience through filters in my mind. As a result, I was spending my life overthinking and overstressing about pretty much everything. No wonder I was convinced I'd personally insulted every dog that barked at me! My understanding of what was going on in my brain was totally out of whack.

Before I go any further, I want you to know, struggling with your thoughts and emotions doesn't make you bad, flawed, or weird; it just makes you a human being. It means, like most of us, you've not been taught how the human brain works, nor have you been given the tools *to work with it*. Up until now, your brain has been unconsciously working against you, which is why you find yourself feeling stuck. Again. And again. And again.

Together, we're going to work to discover what's going on in these brains of ours. I'm going to show you how your brain is holding you back, keeping you locked in self-doubt, worry, and fear. I'm going to reveal what you can do to make yourself feel true peace and joy, and how to understand what's really going on deep down that's preventing it. Hand in hand, we'll begin to treat the root of the tree instead of continuing to just prune the branches.

By the end of this book, you'll be doing the hard work of changing your unhelpful and unproductive thoughts, beliefs, habits, and behaviors so you can finally enjoy life to its full potential.

Clean up your own head

Let me throw a couple of questions at you. Have you ever stopped yourself from negotiating a raise because the thought of rejection was already so overwhelming you couldn't think about it for more than five seconds without wanting to hurl? Have you said "yes" even when you didn't want to because the thought of disappointing someone else made your heart sink with guilt? Have you hesitated to set a much-needed boundary because the emotional disaster you envisioned tied both your stomach and tongue in knots? So often, we are ruled by the fear of the potential, and forget that we are, in fact, in charge of not only our lives, but also our happiness.

As human beings, we tend to *outsource* our happiness. We look to our partner, job, square footage of our house, or salary to determine our level of life satisfaction. And while all of those things may play a part, even when tallied, they don't remotely add up to the whole story.

As we embark on this journey of self-discovery for the sake of self-love, we're going to find that, contrary to popular belief, happiness is not a conditional thing. True happiness has little to do with the things capitalism, the patriarchy, social conditioning, or multibillion-dollar media industries have led us to believe. Peace, joy, and fulfilment are within reach, and there's plenty to go around.

As you work through the ideas and exercises in this book (I promise it won't feel like homework!), you'll learn strategies to take charge of your thoughts and emotions, manage your own happiness, and *drive your own darn bus*. We're going to unpack and put to use the most powerful tool each of us possesses, but none of us fully understand: our brains. Because last time I checked, my brain didn't come with a manual, and I'm willing to bet yours didn't either.

Awaken your emotional strength

If you're looking to change how you think, feel, and show up in your life overnight, you may need to temper your expectations. As annoying as it is, the change process requires small shifts and steps—one at a time. As you journey through this book, you'll build new skills that will take shape and solidify, and then you'll build another one, and another. These skills will ultimately add up to some big transformations that will continue to evolve long after you read the final sentence.

More than anything, this book is about you committing to yourself. Not just once, but every day, hopefully for the rest of your life. And by opening this book today, you've already taken the first step. It's one of the most important things you can do because—and this may be hard to read—you are your only hope. No one else is coming to save you. No one is coming to fix you. No one else can pave the path to realize your dreams. No one is coming... but you.

Sit with this for a second. No other person will ever be as impacted by your life, your choices, your situations, your problems, and your dreams the way you are. Not another soul on this earth can possibly understand as much about you and your happiness as you do. So, if you're stuck waiting for your hero to show up, guess what? It's you. You are the hero of your own story. You are the one who can step in and change your life. You are the one who can unstick you. You have the superpower to make sure you're not just surviving, but *thriving*.

Others may walk with you—everyone needs cheerleaders and champions along the way. But they're not supposed to walk for you. They can't. They have their own journey to navigate. This may seem intimidating at first, but look at it this way: how amazing is it that we each get to go out and create the life we want? On the other side of this journey is true joy and emotional freedom. You may not know it yet, but you deserve to live in a world where you feel good enough exactly as you are. It took me a long time to get there, and I want nothing more than for you to join me.

We all have a story

As a teenager, I was a bit of an outsider. I had friends, but no best friend or clique I could point to and say, "Those are my people!" I felt different than most somehow, like the coolness gene skipped me. And I'm sure it probably didn't help that my conversations with girlfriends often steered away from lipstick and fashion to analyzing the inner workings of human beings and what made them tick (or tock). You guessed it; I was a bit of a psychology nerd—even as a teenager. The good news is, this trait made me a great listener, and people often told me how much better they felt after we'd spoken. So at least I had that.

My infatuation with the human condition began one fateful summer night when I was 14. I even remember the precise moment. I was riding with a friend in the back of her parents' sedan listening to a radio show called "Sex, Lies and Audiotape." It was one of those shows where people called in to ask the therapist host questions about their relationships. As she talked them through their struggles and gave them advice, I knew a version of this was my calling. *There was a job where you could help people overcome their toughest problems and get paid for it?* I was sold right then and there. A few years later, though, I found out that therapists had to have a master's degree in psychology. I distinctly remember the feeling of my stomach doing a free-fall when I learned that information. Convinced a prestigious graduate degree was not an attainable goal for me—the seeds of self-doubt already strong in my psyche after living an adolescence in the shadow of my honor-roll siblings—I dumped the idea altogether.

Instead, I used my listening skills to help others—like the boy 18-year-old me was in love with, but who never loved me back. He'd call *me* to hang out so *we* could talk for hours because his girlfriend didn't understand him the way I did. Oh my young naivete.

After high school, I stumbled my way through the family-mandated undergrad degree with no clear end goal in mind before experimenting with various and unexpected career paths (I'm a pre- and post-natal doula if you're in the market, by the way). But I just couldn't shake the idea of becoming highly trained and educated to help people better understand themselves at a deep, transformational level. Then, on a second fateful evening four years after I graduated university, a single conversation turned my life on a brand-new trajectory and I've never looked back.

I was at my cousin's wedding sitting at a table with his aunt and uncle. I asked them about their daughter, Kim, who I hadn't seen since we were children. Kim wasn't at the wedding, they told me, because she was taking finals for her first year of chiropractic school. At this news, I thought to myself, *Hold on. If whiney little tag-along Cousin Kim can become a chiropractor, then why the heck don't I think I'm capable enough to get that master's degree and pursue my dream to become a clinical therapist?* This was the jolt I didn't know my ego needed to light a fire under my butt after years of stalling. I knew what I needed to do.

I wish I could say this moment of determined resolve was enough to pave a smooth path to my pursuit of becoming a registered therapist. But, alas, the years of doing the bare minimum to pass in my undergrad days caught up with me. I had *a lot* of upgrading to do before I could even apply to grad school. I will say, though, my resolve was unshaken. After four years of upgrading, entrance exams, and applications, the doors of grad school opened for me and I was finally in. And for the first time in a long time (doula days included), where I was, and what I was doing, felt right.

Grad school is where I learned about cognitive therapy, the revolutionary-to-me concept that our thoughts and beliefs create our experience as human beings. My mind was blown. *Blown.* I dove into this area of psychology headfirst. I even had the opportunity to engage in intensive training with Dr David Burns, one of the creators of cognitive therapy, which was like training with a celebrity for me. Shortly after, the concept of mindfulness fell into my lap. Mindfulness deeply resonated with me as I began to explore the idea of learning to *just be* with our feelings and emotions and to allow ourselves an accepting space for our feelings without pushing them away. And when Dr Kristin Neff's research on self-compassion entered my world, it immediately became a key part of my work. Her concept of radically accepting ourselves as perfectly imperfect beings was the lynchpin I didn't even know I'd been looking for, not only professionally, but personally, too. It was as if all the work I'd done on myself was being bolstered and affirmed by the learning I was doing for professional purposes.

And now, 10 years later, here I am—a therapist with the unique privilege of helping to expand the hearts and minds of the incredible clients and students I work with every day. This has never been a job for me. It's been a calling since Rhona Raskin's radio waves drew me in that fateful evening in the back of my friend's mid-size sedan.

How to use this book

I've divided this book into four sections that build on one another, much like you'll be building on yourself as you work through them. In **Part One: How Our Emotions and Thoughts Get into the Driving Seat**, you'll dig deep and find the source of your thoughts and emotions, as well as the lengths we humans often go to in order to avoid them—even though this avoidance is at the root of many internal issues. You'll learn the ABCBO model, which will help you separate your thoughts from your emotions, as well as better understand how they are connected to each and every choice you make.

You'll also see how shame and the ancient, or primitive, brain often work against you. And by the end of this section, you'll know how to properly use your brain as a tool to break down your emotional reactions to any given person or situation (and you'll be practicing, too!).

In **Part Two: Become the Driver of Your Own Emotions**, you'll take on some of your most difficult emotions in greater depth and dive into the minutiae of your mind amid intense emotions. Shame, guilt, stress, anger, anxiety—it's time to learn what these emotions mean to you and how to work through them. (Don't worry, I'm going to teach you how!) You're going to learn how to access your rational mind when you need it so you can respond instead of react—our default setting—when those powerful emotions arise.

Part Three: Become the Driver of Your Own Thoughts tackles the out-of-control thoughts that cause feelings of worthlessness, stress, and disconnection. You may be experiencing destructive thought patterns without even knowing it. Brains are tricky like that. Here, you'll learn to discover the root of your biggest self-worth struggles and create a strong and confident identity from the inside out.

And finally, **Part Four: Become the Driver of Your Own Behaviors** examines self-sabotage through passivity, and how to stop doing it. You'll set boundaries, stop people-pleasing, say "no" clearly yet kindly, and put yourself firmly in the driver's seat of your own darn bus.

In all four sections, you'll find journaling prompts and exercises. I'm not just going to lecture you about changing your life; you're going to use the most powerful machine in your possession to draw up your own roadmap of change: your brain.

So, renew your commitment to yourself, get your brain warmed up, grab yourself a pen and a cup of kombucha (or whatever the cool kids are drinking these days), and let's get started.

PART ONE

HOW YOUR EMOTIONS AND THOUGHTS GET INTO THE DRIVING SEAT

Okay, friend, let's begin with a little emotional self-assessment. Do you tend to cry easily, laugh loudly, and feel deeply? Are you a person who verbally processes your emotions? Or do you bury your feelings deep because you worry about being open and honest even with yourself? Do you find yourself hiding behind an "it's all good" facade even when it's really not? Or are you someone who wears your feelings on your sleeve for all to see?

We all have emotions. We have them all day, every day—it comes with this whole being-human gig. Unfortunately, when our feelings become intense or difficult, it can be overwhelming. If you're anything like me, when you think back on your life, you may realize no one ever explicitly taught you what to do when your anxiety spikes or an intense wave of hot shame washes over you. So, if we never learned or practiced handling big (complex) emotions in healthy ways, then how can we be expected to know what to do with them now? And it's not just emotions, right? Managing our thoughts can also be confusing, to say the least. It's a good thing you're here now.

Remember the time you got into an argument with that other driver who zipped right into the parking spot you'd very clearly been waiting for? I mean, you had your blinker on and everything. And then, hours after it was over, the confrontation was still playing on a loop in your head? Still angry at their audacity, but also ashamed of your outburst? Or that evening you made a joke that fell flat (like, *flat*) when you were out to dinner with friends, and you *could not* stop thinking about the looks on their faces and what they must have thought of you and your stupid remark? Struggle. Bus. If you know what I'm talking about, you also know these thought spirals feel like emotional torture… because they are.

So, if you're with me and you've ever fallen into the thought traps of overthinking, overstressing, and overanalyzing, raise your hand. (Both my hands are raised, by the way.)

Guess what? It doesn't have to be like this.

CHAPTER 1
THE TROUBLE WITH EMOTIONS

Take a moment of reflection and go back in time. Think.

How were emotions handled when you were a child? Did the adults around you talk about feelings or were feelings to be neither seen nor heard? In your home, were a wide range of feelings encouraged and welcomed? Or were difficult feelings shut down or criticized? Chances are, you were taught neither healthy emotional exploration nor expression, as it wasn't until the late 20th century (yep, you read that right) that parenting experts encouraged adults to talk with children about their feelings. It's also possible your experience lies at the other end of the spectrum, where your emotional role models didn't shut down, but the contrary. They dealt with emotions by yelling, raging, gossiping, or—the sneakiest of all—being passive aggressive. Maybe it wasn't one or the other? Maybe it was all of the above happening under one roof?

Although I don't remember emotions being overtly discouraged in our home while I was growing up, I also don't recall them being openly discussed. When you go back in time and think about what implicit and explicit education you received about emotions, I'm guessing you were likely taught to label your emotions as "good" or "bad" in some way. You were probably encouraged to avoid "bad" ones, and even though "good" emotions were allowed, you had to be careful not to feel *too* good, at the risk of feeling self-important or silly—those belong in the "bad" category.

Perhaps you weren't supported when you were upset or crying. Depending upon your gender, or even your family's culture, crying could mean you were being too sensitive, weak, or acting like "a baby." Maybe intense feelings were allowed, but only in very specific conditions and for a very specific amount of time. When natural, human feelings are restricted, ridiculed, or even punished, it shouldn't be surprising that so many of us develop messed-up ideas about what it means to be a human being with deep emotions. This isn't the first time I've wondered how we got through all this and grew up to be remotely functional people.

Because of this mixed messaging, you, like many of us, may naturally engage in unhealthy behaviors when faced with difficult emotions. Let's test it. Have you ever given your partner the silent treatment for leaving the dishes in the sink? Snapped at the barista for taking 35 seconds longer to foam your milk than you had the patience to endure? Or had your entire day ruined because your typically chipper boss was curt with you? I thought that may be the case. Same here. And I'm sure after any of these things happened, you over-analyzed your actions and wondered why you handled the situation the way you did. That's because human emotions are not easy to understand, especially if you were never taught how to understand them.

The ancient brain

According to cultural and societal expectations, we humans are apparently supposed to be rational beings who are *sometimes* emotional, not the other way around, especially if we are to proceed the "right" way through life. And while my left-brained, analytical engineer husband might agree with this theory, my creative, right-brained self can poke quite a few holes in it.

Whether the left-brained people of the world like it or not, many of us spend excessive time and energy dwelling on emotions—both our own and others'. We get caught in our feelings when people fall short of our expectations. When a coworker snubs you, when chaotic family dynamics boil to the surface, or when wondering what our friends—or anyone else for that matter—thinks of you, it's not always easy to keep your cool. Intense emotions make life tough, but the truth is we don't actually have to be dramatically consumed by them. They feel overwhelming and uncontrollable because *we let them feel that way*. In fact, the majority of our behavior is principally motivated by our need for safety and, thus, ultimately, survival.

Seriously. It's (almost) that simple.

You may have previously heard the term "ancient brain"—also known as the survival or primitive brain—and its drive to save us from the predators of prehistoric times, like hungry saber-tooth tigers and moody, often explosive volcanos. This superfast reaction from our non-rational brain kicks in before our rational brain has a chance to apply reason to our circumstances. After centuries, this fight-or-flight instinct continues to be firmly embedded in our physiological systems and is triggered when we perceive a potential threat. Here's the thing, this instinct kicks in to avoid potential pain and danger, like an all-consuming fire or a wild boar. Unfortunately for us 21st-century dwellers, though, it can also kick in when you lose your train of thought while giving a boardroom presentation. This can be tricky and might even cause an embarrassing moment or two, but it has nothing to do with your shortcomings and everything to do with normal, ancient brain function.

This part of the human brain doesn't always know the difference between *real* or *imagined* threats to your survival. Therefore, it's not always able to discern whether you're being aggressively approached by a shady stranger, or passing by a harmless jogger. Even more complexly, the ancient brain can't always understand that being judged by your coworkers for a mediocre workshop isn't an actual threat to your existence, no matter how embarrassed you are. It's true, you cannot die of embarrassment. However, in all these situations, regardless of the presence of a real threat, your fear response is triggered and results in an increased heart rate, shallow breathing, tunnel vision, sweating, and so on.

Your ego and its role

I can't write a book about taking charge of your life without discussing one of the most basic aspects of each and every one of us: ego. I bet your stomach flipped when you read that word. Why? Because when we think of the word "ego" we often picture someone with an inflated one. Maybe an angry businessman yelling at an underling who crossed him the wrong way or a high-and-mighty actress laughing at a reporter for getting facts about her incorrect. These images aren't wrong, but they're over-the-top examples of what an unchecked ego looks like.

At its most basic, your ego is your sense of who you are. During childhood, when our brains are the most spongy and hungry for learning, our thoughts and opinions (read: sense) of ourselves are created. As we learn and grow physically, we also learn what we need to do in order to receive love and acceptance. Our brains are on a mission to understand how to be "good enough" to get our needs met. Each time we behave a certain way and are rewarded with love, attention, or even with material things, our desire to continue that behavior is solidified. Add to that the fact that we are consistently told things about ourselves that become woven into our identity. For example, if we're told we're inquisitive, naughty, motivated, or even silly, chances are we embodied those things. All of these beliefs and behaviors interlace, creating a unique sense of self—our ego. We take ownership of that sense of self, as we should! However, sometimes that ownership can become problematic.

Ego is a tricky thing. When we have a good relationship with our ego (which many call having it "in check"), it's easy to receive feedback and to learn from others because nothing shakes that sense of self. For example, if your ego is heavily reliant on your unmatched motivation and your ego is in check, you'll have no problem integrating new tools to help with your motivation if and when it takes a small dip. If your ego isn't in check, you might feel angry when someone suggests taking a look at a tool they've been using for motivation. Why? Because suggesting that you could improve in an area you feel is integral to who you are threatens your sense of self. Raise your hand if this has happened to you.

Same here.

Avoidance strategies

When our ancient brain is active and we are faced with big emotions—no matter what emotions they are—our natural, primitive instinct is to distance ourselves from the distress as quickly as possible. And, yes, this includes those sneaky little threats to our ego. However, because we can't physically run away from feelings, we often opt to numb, avoid, repress, buffer, or diffuse them by whatever means necessary, even if only temporarily. This is where things start to get a little messy. Let's review some common avoidance strategies you may have employed in the past:

- **Avoiding people and things:** Have you ever stayed home instead of socializing because you're worried about potential anxiety you may feel if, while out with others, you commit a faux pas of some kind? Or perhaps you talk yourself out of trying new things, like checking out the new yoga studio everyone's raving about, because you don't want to be the awkward, inflexible person in the corner. Or maybe you remain stuck in a career you don't enjoy because you've already convinced yourself you'll fail if you try anything else.
- **Repressing:** Ever ignored what you're really feeling so you don't rock the boat or pretend you're A-OK when you're really not?
- **Over-blaming yourself:** Caught yourself obsessing over how terrible, wrong, or deficient you are when things go

poorly? You're so busy beating yourself up, you don't have the space to mindfully reflect on how to improve next time.
- **Over-blaming others:** The art of spending so much time focused on others' wrongdoings there is no space left to process what you're actually feeling and why.
- **Numbing or buffering:** A quick fix that feels good in the moment but makes you feel a whole lot worse later. Cut to shoveling down an entire box of doughnuts post-break-up, social-media bingeing after an argument, or drinking an entire bottle of wine to de-stress on a Friday night. Or worse, a Monday night. Woof.

Humans have become adept in our ability to avoid, repress, project, and buffer our emotions with substances, shopping, eating, social media, gossiping—anything to get away from our uncomfortable emotions as quickly as we can. This all may be maladaptive, but it's important to note we're not being stupid or unevolved when we engage in unhealthy coping strategies. We use these methods because they work in some capacity, in addition to helping our brains manage difficult emotions and find the immediate relief it's looking for.

Every behavior has a purpose—every single thing you do, every coping mechanism you employ—is for a reason. The problem is the relief you feel when you use these kinds of strategies is short-lived. Often, they create more problems for our future selves later on, so not only is the root cause of the uncomfortable emotion unresolved, we've compounded the issue in our attempt to feel better. Messy, huh?

Another way humans attempt to offset difficult emotions is by reacting to them. Imagine your unresolved emotions are like water simmering on the stove. You try to keep the lid on, and perhaps it merely simmers for a while. But as the heat turns up, the pressure becomes too much, and our unaddressed emotions boil over. Have you ever yelled at your partner for forgetting to take out the trash when you could have just reminded them? Or screamed at your kids for leaving a mess in the living room instead of simply asking them to tidy up? Or aggressively cut someone off in traffic because you've reached your limit for incompetent driving? When you're walking around with a constant simmer of unprocessed emotions, it only takes a degree or two for your emotional pot to boil over and flip the lid right off.

If you've never been taught how to work through your emotions in a healthy way, your default will always be to revert to your more primitive instincts and rid yourself of emotional burdens in the quickest, easiest—but often not the most productive—way possible. We'll get into this more later, but before we move on, I have one request: please do not judge yourself for the coping methods you've been using, whether it's one or all of those listed. You're just doing the best you can with what you have in this moment in the absence of learning a better way.

Stick with me. You'll get there.

Feel and deal

Western culture puts excessive stock into the idea of "feeling good" all the time, which often makes people feel like they're doing something wrong when life isn't unending sunshine and rainbow unicorns. However, you now know you've likely been dealt a bad hand when it comes to knowing how to properly sort through and respond to difficult emotions… in addition to the fact that life is not, in fact, unending sunshine and unicorns. With that, we don't need the added shame of thinking there's something wrong for having less than happy and positive emotions every once in a while. So, let's cut right through the shame and talk about how normal it is to be a human being with human feelings—the good, the bad, and even the ugly ones—and then get to the "how to sort them out" part.

First things first: the journey toward your emotionally intelligent self begins with doing something that may sound counterintuitive: learning how to *have* your feelings. You're not going to "get over" them or "control" them because you can't.

Instead, you're going to *be with them* so they can stop controlling you. Simple as that.

I promise you, this practice alone will make a huge difference in your life. The act of allowing yourself to truly experience your feelings without getting stuck in the cycle of avoidance or reaction will help you stop the personal emotional rollercoaster you've been trying to offboard. In the next chapter, you're going to learn how to make it happen.

TAKEAWAYS

- Most of us don't actually know how to deal with our difficult emotions because we've never been encouraged to allow them.
- Most of our actions are determined by our desire to move toward pleasure and avoid pain or potential discomfort.
- We all have go-to strategies we use to avoid, buffer, or project difficult feelings.

Journal prompt: What (situations, people, experiences) do I avoid because I think I won't be able to manage the emotions that may arise?

CHAPTER 2
EMBRACING YOUR EMOTIONS

Take a moment and ask yourself: *What if I could safely feel any feeling? What if I knew that, no matter what, I could feel rejection, sadness, hurt, or disappointment and get through it just fine?*

I'm serious. What if you could feel *any* feeling and be okay after? I'm not saying it would feel great, but what if you could handle any one of your emotions? What would change? What would happen if you *knew* you could navigate any uncomfortable feeling?

What would you do?

What are emotions?
Let's start by taking a closer look at emotions.

All emotions exist for a reason—even the uncomfortable ones. For starters, I don't like to label emotions as "good" or "bad," as this casts judgment on both our emotions and on ourselves for having them, which isn't helpful.

For example, people sometimes categorize emotions that indicate something is not right or dangerous as "bad." With this, we were also taught to avoid these kinds of emotions. (Heaven forbid we aren't positive every second of our lives.) So, instead of wondering what's going on and asking ourselves why we're

DRIVE YOUR OWN DARN BUS

feeling what we're feeling, we try to diminish the discomfort via those go-to avoidance strategies we talked about in Chapter 1.

But here's the truth: these so-called "negative" emotions aren't the terrible, threatening, intolerable things we build them up to be. All emotions are, quite simply, *a generally benign sensation in our bodies*. In and of themselves, emotions are not immediately threatening or dangerous. Uncomfortable? Yes. Intolerable? Not really. They are merely biological states associated with your nervous system brought on by neuro-physical changes caused by the release of different hormones and neurotransmitters. They can show up as any contactless physiological sensation, like your stomach "flipping," your chest "tightening," your head feeling "hot," or your skin "tingling."

The words we use to identify our emotions, like angry, anxious, sad, happy, and joyful, identify a particular combination of sensations. That's it. That's all they are.

For example, take anxiety. Anxiety is often associated with physiological feelings like your stomach twisting or flipping, a racing heart, and a tight sensation in the chest. You know why? This combination of neurological impulses is often the way many people experience anxiety. Anger, on the other hand, is generally associated with a hot head or face, a tense stomach, and a tight jaw. Why? Same reason. Take another moment and think about all the things you've done to avoid and offset these combinations of non-threatening, not even actually painful, sensations in your body.

If you've never paid close attention when small children experience emotions, you should next time you have the chance. It's fascinating. For the most part, they haven't learned how to hide or repress their feelings yet, so their emotions are on full display in all their glory. When kids feel something, they *feel* it. They yell, they scream, they stomp, they cry, they laugh, they skip, they dance, they play, they squeal—they *feel*. We lose a lot of that as we get older—which is not always such a bad thing... I'm not sure a grown-up stomping around and screaming on the sidewalk because they missed their bus is the most productive reaction, but there are parts of our learned emotional repression that are causing us more harm than good.

EXERCISE: HOW TO IDENTIFY WHAT YOU'RE FEELING—"THE COLOR BALL"

Now that you've had it broken down intellectually, it's time to start practicing feeling and identifying your emotions with the "Color Ball" exercise. If you struggle to even identify your emotions, this is a wonderful starting place for you. By the way, don't feel badly if you do. Many people, no matter their background, find emotion identification challenging, especially if understanding their feelings wasn't at the forefront of their childhood conversations.

Here's your assignment: Over the next day or two, whenever you have a feeling—*any feeling*—pause and pay attention. When you stop to experience the emotion, think about it as a soft, squishy ball sitting inside you. Then ask yourself, *What color ball is this ball?* and log the first color that enters your mind. Once you have the color, think about the feeling you would most likely associate with it. For example, red is often anger or frustration; blue tends to be sadness or hurt; yellow might be anxiety, etc. Write these items in your journal or somewhere you can refer to later. Whatever "feeling words" and emotions you attach to each color in your head will help you develop more adept skills to understand the feelings you're feeling.

There are no right or wrong answers here. Your feelings are your feelings, and that's quite alright, I promise.

Alarm bells

Here's what so many people don't understand and the thing self-help books never tell you about emotions: we cannot truly control them in the way most people define the word "control."

Often, when clients finally book an appointment with me, they've exhausted all of their available emotion-controlling options and they've reached the end of their rope. They tell me they've been focusing on positive thoughts and good vibes. Many of them have tried forcing their emotions out by yelling at themselves when they're struggling, telling themselves to "STOP FEELING THIS WAY!" And you know if you've ever tried that one—which I definitely have—how well that works. Meaning it doesn't work at all.

You can't *stop* yourself from feeling angry, hurt, jealous, or insecure by telling the feeling to stop. Feelings can't be wished away with positivity or forced away by yelling at yourself. Your feelings don't appear without a reason, so making them disappear isn't quite that easy.

Think of your feelings like a smoke alarm. You can't just turn off the smoke alarm and assume the problem has vanished. Like a smoke alarm, your emotions are telling you something you should probably pay attention to. While there's no guarantee it's sounding off because your emotional house is on fire, it's not ringing for no reason. And like an actual smoke alarm, looking into why it's blaring in the first place is a good idea.

Are you upset because the criticism you received at work is making you question whether you will ever be promotable? Are you insecure because your micromanaging boss was speaking highly of your colleague and you internalized this to mean they don't value you? Are you hurt because your friend didn't text you back for days and you now think your friendship is one-sided? Are you angry because your ever-critical mother commented on your weight, and it triggered feelings of shame? When an emotion arises, it's okay (read: healthy) to ask yourself, *Okay, what's happening here? Why is my alarm going off? Why am I feeling this way, really?*

You can try to escape the alarm—oh, the things we do to escape—but, best-case scenario, if we just cover over the alarm it will only fade to a dull ringing in the background temporarily until it's triggered again, or you pay attention to what's setting it off in the first place.

Bad feelings are good

So, how do we learn to deal with the smoke alarm, escape-triggering, troublesome emotions? Well, the first thing we need to do is practice fully feeling them. I know it may sound silly that we need to learn and practice *feeling* our feelings, but it's true.

By now, you may be rolling your eyes because you think you're "feeling" already. I often hear people say, "I constantly worry my boss is going to realize I don't deserve my position because I don't actually know what I'm doing," or, "I get anxious about whether I said the right thing when I was out with friends and wonder if I accidentally offended someone all the time." However, *having* difficult emotions, no matter how frequently, is not the same as allowing yourself the space to feel them. Being stuck in a cycle of emotional turmoil is not the same as processing emotional pain or discomfort.

As you travel this journey with me, I'm going to teach you how possible it is to properly process and feel difficult feelings. You don't have to get stuck or fear your difficult feeling—and I can bet you'll find it's not nearly as terrible as you think to feel terrible.

Think it with me: *It's not bad to have "bad" feelings.*

One more time for the people in the back: **It's not bad to have "bad" feelings**.

Want some more good news? Once your brain understands terrible feelings are nothing to fear, when you do feel terrible it'll feel *less* terrible. Less. Not more. Your emotions, including the ones that set off every single alarm, are not right, wrong, bad, or good. They exist for a reason and, if you want to be the driver of your mind and emotions, you have to learn how to have them all.

Pushback

I would be remiss if I didn't warn you about something you will experience on the journey to drive your own bus. When you first allow yourself to really feel, there is no magic fairy dust that makes it instantly pleasant. Feeling sounds simple and easy, but it's not. Your brain and body aren't used to it; they're used to the old emotional freak-out-and-combust, and they're *really good at it*.

Your brain, like all human brains, is a creature of habit, and regardless of whether the habit is helpful, healthy, or otherwise, the human brain likes predictability. When you start changing the routine on your brain by, for example, altering your emotional responses, it's going to push back. Guaranteed. This resistance is not a sign you're doing something wrong; it's just your brain's natural response to change.

Resistance can take many forms. As you step into a new way of relating to your brain, watch for thoughts like, *This is too hard*, or, *I can't do this*, or, *This is going to take too long*. Honestly, if those thoughts show up, take it as a sign of progress. It means you are starting to change, and your change-averse brain is pulling out all the stops to bring you back to the status quo. And though it may not quite know it yet, it will get better and easier, and your brain will come around.

How to feel your feelings

We've already talked about step one of this process: identify what emotions you're feeling as they surface. Not too bad, right? Hopefully, you've been working through the "Color Ball" exercise we discussed earlier. If so, you have probably noticed some emotions are easier to identify, accept, and own (joy, excitement, and love) than others (shame, fear, or vulnerability). Perhaps you've noticed, like I have, that emotions we consider negative are tricky to pin down and even harder to process.

So, let's start there. To process an emotion you can't quite name, start brainstorming descriptive words about your physiology and thoughts. What does your body feel like when you feel it? It might go something like, "Right now, my stomach feels like it's flipping, my jaw is tense, and it's like there's a weight on my chest." The name of this combination of sensations is likely "anxiety."

Another example could be, "I have a sense of tunnel vision, a lump in my throat, and a sinking feeling in my stomach. I am repeating negative thoughts about myself in my head." This experience is probably something related to "shame."

That's it.

Describing the emotion with whatever language you have explicitly demonstrates to your brain a few things: you know what the emotion is, you know that it's there and, crucially, you're able to listen and attend to the emotion. These components ultimately lead to the simple and powerful act of *acceptance.* You're not avoiding, repressing, or working yourself up about your feelings. You are simply acknowledging them. Good for you! You are now officially processing instead of avoiding or reacting to your feelings. How does it feel?

When you accept and allow yourself to experience your feelings, your brain begins to understand it doesn't need to continue blasting the alarm. You're telling your brain the problem is a burnt piece of toast, not a house fire, and you can deal with it.

Acceptance doesn't mean you enjoy or even want to experience whatever you're feeling; acceptance means you understand you are not in danger, you're experiencing discomfort in your body. And after all we've been through, you and I both know discomfort is survivable.

EXERCISE: FEELING YOUR EMOTIONS

It's time to practice your emotional identification and processing together. We are taking the "Color Ball" exercise and going one step further.

For the next two days, whenever you're feeling anxiety, sadness, or anger, I want you to notice how it's showing up in your body and record it. In your journal, a notepad, or even the Notes app on your phone, record exactly how the emotion feels in your body. If you've ever practiced mindfulness, you can think of this exercise like a body scan. Pause and search for where you feel the emotion. Your notes might look something like:

Time	Where do I feel this emotion?	What does this emotion feel like?	What am I feeling?
10am	Chest	Racing heart, breathing fast	Anxiety
1pm	Stomach, throat	Sinking feeling in my stomach and some tension in my throat	Sadness
8pm	Chest, head, eyes	Tightness in my chest, hotness in my head, tunnel vision in my eyes	Anger

This process of manually logging your emotions and what they feel like will etch these experiences into your brain in a way solely thinking about something cannot.

You may be wondering what happens if you're not sure what exactly you're feeling. Don't worry; that's okay, too. If you find this exercise is a struggle, stay with "The Color Ball" and practice categorizing your feelings for a while more. Feeling your feelings is the imperative first step in preventing your emotions from consuming you, and, like all good things, it takes time. Here is a blank template you can put to use when you're ready!

Time	Where do I feel this emotion?	What does this emotion feel like?	What am I feeling?

Stepping on the brakes

This seemingly simple process of naming and describing your emotions as they physically present themselves will help prevent emotional spirals and overwhelm. It helps us "step on the brakes" of our emotional reactions. And now that you know emotions are just harmless physical sensations in your body, you're likely wondering *why* they cause so many problems in our lives. Why do they have the potential to ruin an entire day or put us in a funk for weeks? Well, it's not your emotions; they just get a bad rap. The real problem lies with—are you ready for it?—our thoughts.

TAKEAWAYS

- Emotions are just physiological sensations in your body.
- *It's not bad to have bad feelings.* (This isn't the last time you'll read this.)
- We can properly *feel* our feelings when we take the time to describe and identify them.
- Truly *feeling* emotions may be uncomfortable, but we are okay.

Journal prompt: Why might I be resistant to feeling my feelings? What do I think might happen if I do?

CHAPTER 3

THE TROUBLE WITH THOUGHTS

Although most of us may not realize it, we humans traverse through life far more stressed and anxious than is necessary. We live day in and day out feeling overwhelmed and worried, often never taking a step back and really asking ourselves what's *really* stressing us out, worrying us, or causing that panicky heartbeat.

Now, of course there are times when the why is obvious. Days when you have a million things to do in 24 hours (fewer if you plan to sleep), or when you have no idea how you're going to meet your big deadline, are no-brainers. We are also often aware of anticipatory anxiety about things like large family gatherings with misogynistic uncles and passive-aggressive parents, or financial stressors like stretching your budget for birthdays and weddings.

However, there are also times when troublesome feelings just exist in us without a clear trigger. This is really where it gets tough, right? When you feel generally stressed, anxious, or depleted without a seemingly good reason, it can be a struggle to understand the source. In situations like these, it's tempting to become judgmental of ourselves, but we're going to work on that together!

EMOTIONS DIARY

I know you've been working on identifying your emotions and connecting them to your physiological responses (I hope it's going well!). Building on the exercises from the previous chapter about identifying and processing your feelings, it's time to start being consistent with logging your feelings. This is especially helpful if you've been feeling overwhelmed, upset, or anxious without a clear understanding of the trigger or source. First, use the skills you've been building to identify the feeling. Then, ask yourself what was or is going on in your life, head, or environment. What's it all about? Why is it there?

You might record it in your journal like this:

Sunday 12pm	Feeling stressed	That stupid train was delayed and made me late for my hair appointment. I hate being late!
Sunday 3pm	Feeling upset	Carla said that my new hairstyle didn't suit me.
Sunday 7pm	Feeling overwhelmed	My boss keeps emailing me with more tasks for next week and I can't possibly get them all done.
Monday 7am	Feeling anxious	I often wake up with a sinking feeling on Mondays but am not sure why.
Monday 12pm	Feeling hurt	A group of colleagues went for lunch and didn't invite me.
Monday 6pm	Feeling angry	My partner texted to say they were going out for a drink and wouldn't be home until late.
Tuesday 3am	Feeling panic	I woke up in the night sweating and my heart was racing, but am not sure exactly why.

Keep in mind that there are no right or wrong feelings. This exercise is here to reinforce what you've already started: noticing, processing, and recording the situations that stir up emotions in you and what those emotions are. Start with the goal of continuing this exercise for another two days and go from there.

The thoughts behind the feelings

As this exercise helps you become more aware of your external and internal emotional triggers—activities, experiences, situations, people, conversations, etc.—can you see any emerging patterns? Do your unpleasant feelings seem to center around your workday or your home environment? Do they happen at predictable times throughout the day? Can you see trends in events or people who tend to prompt specific feelings? Is the cause for some of your feelings still a mystery?

Okay. Brace yourself. What if I told you that your emotional reactions are not actually fully linked to your experiences or the people around you? Well, dear fellow human, that's what I'm telling you. Your environment and other people don't cause all your feelings at all. The late train, awkward conversations, and rude people have much less to do with your stress, anxiety, or upset feelings. Ready to identify the culprit? *Your thoughts!* Yes, your thoughts connected to all these scenarios (and the hundreds of others we experience every day) are creating the real problem.

Yep. It's true. *Your* brain (i.e., the brain) is responsible for every uncomfortable feeling you experience. Your happiness, shame, hurt, worry, and anger—those physiological reactions we talked through before—are not actually responsible for anything. They are reactions to the conscious and unconscious thoughts running through your head.

Allow me to explain a little more.

First off, let's clear the air. I'm not saying you're imagining your feelings out of nothing. Your boss put a heap of extra tasks on your desk, you weren't included in the office posse lunch plan, your friend definitely did criticize your new hairstyle, and the 40-minute traffic delay certainly made you late for work.

However, when things happen and we *interpret* those experiences in a particular way, we often place meaning on them far beyond the simple facts. For example, if I trip and fall, the facts are just that: I tripped and then fell. As humans, though, we'll often add on meanings like, "Eesh, I can't even walk. What's wrong with me?" or, "Oh good. Everyone thinks I'm an idiot now." This is completely normal, as humans are meaning-making machines. All the same, we *give* experiences meaning. The experiences themselves just *are*. You have a perspective (read: thoughts) about what happens or doesn't happen, and your interpretation of the event or non-event is what creates your emotional reaction.

I'll share an example from my own life. Last week, when someone cut me off in traffic, my body tensed and my blood pressure rose, so I hit the horn. I was annoyed. But why did I feel this way? Well, because I immediately began a narrative about the driver being a selfish jerk who thought their commute was more important than mine. Fair enough, right?

You know what's fascinating, though? Someone else in the exact same situation may have felt embarrassed instead of annoyed. When they were cut off, they could have felt heat wash over their face accompanied by a sinking feeling in their stomach. This isn't because their experience was different; it's because their *thoughts* were different. They might be mentally narrating the situation with something like, *Oh my gosh, was I driving so badly I pissed that person off? I feel so stupid!*

Your turn. Imagine the next time you pause your reading to look at your phone, you see an email from your boss with the subject line: *We need to talk.*

What would your feelings and thoughts be? Here we go.

If you're **Person A**, you might react with worried feelings. Perhaps your stomach would feel like it had dropped to your feet. If you're **Person B**, perhaps you could have annoyed feelings, which may show up in your body like lukewarm anger—still a hot face and head, but it's no raging fire of hell. And **Person C**? Well, you just might feel excited, going pleasantly lightheaded while your stomach flips with happy potential.

Persons A, **B**, and **C** might react to the exact same experience with three completely different feelings. This is what I mean when I say our thoughts, not our feelings, create the majority of our emotional experiences.
Person A felt worried because they were *thinking* something like, *Oh crap, what did I do wrong? This doesn't sound good.* **Person B** felt annoyed because they were *thinking* along the lines of, *Not another thing—why won't they leave me alone? Don't they know how much I have on my plate already?* And **Person C** was excited because they were *thinking* thoughts like, *I've been putting in long hours and working extra hard lately—I bet they're finally going to give me that promotion!*

See how it works?

Our personal interpretation of what we experience creates our personal meaning, which, in turn, creates our personal feelings. This principle is why individuals can have opposite reactions to the same exact event. A 40-minute transportation delay won't create annoyance and stress for every waiting passenger on the platform. If someone's thoughts were, *Perfect. I was dreading that meeting. Now that I'll get out of it, I can just review the minutes*, they'll be happy as can be to wait the extra time.

Because we're not always fully conscious of the thoughts and beliefs prompting our responses, we often don't realize our part in our own emotions. They rise inside us, seemingly out of our control, when we neglect to understand what's really going on in our brains.

The story we tell ourselves

Renowned psychiatrist David Burns, one of the creators of Cognitive Behavioral Therapy (CBT), was my introduction to the concept of thought work. His book, *Feeling Good*, was the first book I read on the subject and to this day, it's one of the most popular and well-known psychology-based self-help books. Burns, along with Donald Meichenbaum, Aaron T Beck, and Albert Ellis, brought to the mainstream the idea that our thoughts are the source of our feelings. Meichenbaum calls human beings *Homo narrans*, or story-makers, because we each create the narrative of our own life. He explored the concept of the entire human emotional experience being built around the stories we tell ourselves about other people, the world, ourselves, the way things should be, and what it all means.

When clients or students come to me hoping to get "unstuck," I give them the same homework assignment almost every time: Between now and the next session, pay attention to your thoughts when you're feeling sad, mad, rejected, hurt, or angry. Just pay attention to the thoughts in your head in moments when you notice a difficult feeling arise. When they come back the next week, their feelings are backed by a story.

EXERCISE: WHERE DO OUR EMOTIONS COME FROM?

Pause and take a moment to remember the last difficult emotion you had. How did you know you were having a difficult feeling and what did it feel like? By now, you're a budding expert at this part.

Now, as always, we're going to build on our skills. Think about those feelings as an indicator to pivot to your mind. When you notice a difficult emotion, use it as a prompt to examine your thoughts and, like usual, write them down. Aim for three or four entries daily for two or three days. Your log might look like this (see opposite):

Activating event (what happened)	Thoughts and beliefs (story about what happened)	Emotional consequence (how I felt)
I missed my train so I'll be late for work.	My boss is going to think I'm irresponsible.	Anxious
My mother called and commented that I forgot my aunt's birthday.	My mom thinks I'm incompetent.	Angry

Get familiar with seeking out your thoughts when emotions are running high before you move on to the next stage. Since the average human has about 6,000 thoughts a day, you'll have plenty of opportunities to engage in this process. Don't worry, though, you don't need to pay attention to all of them, but those three or four are a good place to start.

A few years ago, I got an email from a student criticizing me for treating them unfairly. Initially, I felt angry at the criticism because I think of myself as a considerate and fair leader, but then my anger turned into shame because my next thought was that if she didn't like something I'd done, it must mean I'm not as good of a leader as I thought I was. As I thought further, though, I understood my student was creating her own narrative about what my actions meant about her, or her own ideas about how a leader should or should not lead, and that's what was creating her anger. In the end, it wasn't actually about me at all, despite my initial thoughts and feelings.

Another example from my life happened a few months ago. I messaged a friend on a night I'd been feeling lonely and disconnected: *Are you free tonight to meet in the community garden for a drink and a visit?* She messaged me back: *Oh sorry, I have other plans already.* I immediately felt hurt, so I ventured into my mind and peered into my thoughts. Upon reflection, my mental drama was something like, *I guess I'm not all that important to her, or maybe even all that important in general.* Having been practicing this skill set for a while now, I was able to catch this thought quickly and reassure myself that there was no actual truth to my internal narrative. I'd sent a last-minute request, and people are often busy or tired by the end of the day. "No, thanks" does not equate to personal rejection.

Here's the chart I would have drawn up around these situations:

Activating event *What happened*	Thoughts and beliefs *Story about what happened*	Emotional consequence *Feelings about what happened*
Email from student	Wow—I must be a bad leader for someone to be so upset.	Shame
Message from my friend saying she couldn't meet me	My friend obviously has better things to do with her time and doesn't care about me as much as I do about her.	Hurt

Where do our thoughts come from?

Your brain is constantly trying to make sense of the world around you, which is why it creates those stories to make sense of everything and everyone, including how you fit into it all. The foundation of our thinking about situations, interactions, and experiences was formed when we were young and our brains were learning how to think through direct teaching, examples, observation, and the general absorption of the world around us.

Essentially, the thoughts in your head are just a string of words in your brain you picked up somewhere or from someone along the way. A sentence that your mind believes to be true. Unfortunately (or maybe fortunately, depending on your perspective), your thoughts do not necessarily paint an accurate portrait of reality. They are not always facts, therefore they are not always true. Even more unfortunately, we usually think they are.

EXERCISE: THIS THOUGHT IS NOT A TRUTH

Before you jump in and try to start doing a complete overhaul on all your unhelpful thoughts, start by simply observing thoughts as "just thoughts." The next time you feel an emotion in your body (since you're so good at it now), take a stroll around your mind on a thought-discovery mission. When you run into one, say to yourself, *This is just a thought. It is not necessarily a fact, a truth, or the only way to interpret what's happening. It's an option, but not a conclusion.*

Thoughts become habits

When you notice resistance to your mantra that thoughts might not be the truth—you already know your brain is going to fight change—put yourself in the shoes of someone else in a similar situation. Your brain wants your thoughts to be absolute truth, but is it certain someone else in this situation would be thinking the exact same thing? Remember the "we need to talk" email?

Just because you're thinking something doesn't mean you're right. You've just thought these kinds of thoughts for so long that your brain thinks you are.

When you find your brain clinging to these thoughts as truths, ask yourself what will happen if you choose an alternate interpretation (or different thoughts). Will you be okay? If you detach from your automatic thoughts, will any harm come to you? Imagine if the alternate thoughts you chose weren't anxiety-producing, stress-inducing, hurt-inflicting. How would your life change?

Once you start to unpack your unconscious mind in this way, you will become more aware of the troubling thoughts behind your difficult emotions. And in doing so, you will learn to change your entire human experience.

TAKEAWAYS

- Our *thoughts* cause our biggest problems, not our emotions.
- We now know it's our *thoughts* about our experiences that create our feelings (i.e., how we interpret situations and what we tell ourselves these interpretations mean).
- Our emotional experience is generally the result of our internal narrative.
- Our thoughts are *not* necessarily true.
- Most of our thoughts are actually habits.

Journal prompt: When I'm feeling anxious or insecure, what kinds of thought patterns run through my mind? Why those thoughts? Where might they have come from?

CHAPTER 4
THOUGHTS CREATE FEELINGS, FEELINGS CREATE BEHAVIORS

For some, finding the interconnection of your thoughts and feelings may still feel like a big jump you're not quite ready to take, while others may be all-in. Either way, let's come back to these simple—yet not always easy—reminders:

1. A thought is simply an interpretation—not a fact.
2. A feeling is a sensation in our body—not a threat.
3. More often than not, our *thoughts* create our feelings.

I hope you're beginning to see how your thoughts pop up and cause your emotional reaction as you work your way through the exercises. One of my favorite—very true—sayings comes to mind when I reflect on this idea, "We don't see the world the way it is; we see the world from where we are."

Although we walk through life assuming we see things clearly, we are totally unaware we're looking through our own individual windshields. But unfortunately, they're scratched, tinted, and smudged because of everything we've been driving through. We think we're seeing clearly, but our own biases, conditioning, and influences mar our gaze at every turn and our resulting perceptions are skewed by our pre-existing internal world.

Consider a scenario in which you and your partner are in the throes of an unresolved fight. You've been angrily silent for five minutes, and then you get a text from a friend canceling your weekend plans. At this juncture, you might be quick to think something negative like, *See! Everyone's against me and no one cares about me*. However, if you received the same text at the end of a great date with your partner, you more easily think, *That's too bad, but I understand. She has a lot going on right now.*

Our thoughts and, subsequently, our feelings are influenced by so many factors—which is why investigating them is so important.

The ABCBO model

As we take more steps into the world of understanding our thoughts and emotions, I modified psychologist Albert Ellis's ABC model to create the ABCBO model. This little brain-changer gives you the tools to understand your thoughts and how they are influencing not only your feelings, but also your actions. We'll start with the ABC part of the model—which is essentially what you've been uncovering during your practice of recognizing the connection between your perceptions, thoughts, and feelings:

A = **A**ctivating Event

B = **B**elief (Your thoughts about and your interpretation of **A**)

C = **C**onsequential Emotions (What feelings happen after **A** and **B** compound)

Activating Event (**A**) + Belief (**B**) = Consequential Emotions (**C**)

Identifying the ABC

Imagine Heather and her family head to her mother's house for a holiday dinner. During the visit, her young children are running around and being generally unruly. At some point,

Heather's mother says, "You know, the kids are kind of acting crazy. What's going on? You never behaved like this when you were little. I always made sure you were quiet and polite." Heather is incensed.

Now, in straightforward terms, Heather's kids were running around and then Heather's mom made a comment about it. But why does Heather feel angry? Would you feel angry? Or perhaps you'd feel sad? Or would you laugh it off with an eye roll?

Let's head to the ABC chart. If Heather was upset, she would probably say the "A" was her mother's criticism, and because of that she felt angry and hurt.

However, you know by now it's not this simple. What if Heather was working on becoming the driver of her own bus, and perhaps didn't hear it as criticism? Before we infuse the emotion into any part of the ABC, including our descriptive language, we need to neutralize the activating event as much as possible. Describing the event in an objectively neutral way helps us see how different people (or even us on different days) might interpret the same situation in completely different ways. Making it a practice to work through events like this can calm your own emotional reactions quickly.

When we neutralize our description of "A" for Heather's ABC chart, it might look like this:

Activating Event (A)	Belief or Thoughts (B)	Consequential Emotions (C)
Mom made a comment about the kids		

When we add the "B," we get:

Activating Event (A)	Belief or Thoughts (B) *What Heather thought*	Consequential Emotions (C) *What Heather felt*
Mom made a comment about the kids	*Mom criticizing my parenting means I'm a terrible parent.*	

Which makes Heather feel her "C":

Activating Event (A)	Belief or Thoughts (B) What Heather thought	Consequential Emotions (C) What Heather felt
Mom made a comment about the kids	Mom criticizing my parenting means I'm a terrible parent.	Anger, shame

The emotion only makes sense once we look at the "B" column and understand the story Heather told herself about her mother's words. Technically, the "A" isn't about criticizing Heather's parenting—the "A" is simply the string of words Heather's mother said. Technically, Heather's activating event was merely words until she made up a story about what it meant.

Depending upon our perception, it's easy to think of such a comment as judgmental and identify it as the source of Heather's shame. However, her emotion is not actually caused by her mother's words, but by what she thinks and believes to be "true" about what her mother said.

Let's explore some other reactions Heather could have had, depending upon her perspective and the story she told herself in that moment.

Activating Event (A)	Belief or Thoughts (B) What Heather thought	Consequential Emotions (C) What Heather felt
Mom made a comment about the kids	Mom criticizing my parenting means I'm a terrible parent.	Anger, shame
Mom made a comment about the kids	Mom shouldn't be nosing into business that isn't hers.	Annoyance
Mom made a comment about the kids	Mom is commenting on how her parenting style and mine are different.	Calm

Look back at some of the patterns you noticed after Chapter 2 when we talked about noticing what tends to upset you. See if you can identify and neutralize the activating event for a given situation—the "A" you believed was the root cause of your feelings. Remember, the more you neutralize your description of your **A**ctivating event, the easier it will be to identify which of your **B**eliefs led to your **C**onsequential emotion.

A neutralized "A" is not *I live with a slob* when you arrive home from work and your roommate's breakfast dishes are piled on the kitchen counter. Rather, it would be something like *My roommate left dishes on the kitchen counter.* A neutralized "A" is, *My boss sent me an email to remind me to finish a task*, not, *My overbearing boss thinks I'm a complete idiot.* A neutralized "A" is, *My mom said words about how often I call* vs *My dysfunctional mom laid a big guilt trip on me about how often I should be calling her.* The neutral event description is an objective statement, as if it's written by someone not emotionally attached to the situation. Hard, I know, but possible—and so freeing!

Behaviors (B) and Outcomes (O)

Are you starting to recognize how to separate the activating event from your emotional reaction by taking the time to pull out the thoughts caught in the middle? Well, now that you've got the ABC down, let's round out the ABCBO model with the "B" and "O":

B = **B**ehavior (What you do after you feel the **C**onsequential emotion)

O = **O**utcome (What happens after your **B**ehavior)

Did you love those "Choose Your Own Adventure" books from the 1980s like I did? I'd get to a cliffhanger and would be prompted to turn to page 87 if I wanted to challenge the warlock or head to page 99 if I wanted to explore the castle. Being the master of the story was amazing, wasn't it? (If you don't know what I'm talking about, I guess you were objectively cooler than me. But that's okay!) Either way, guess what? Your life is truly your personal "Choose Your Own Adventure" story! *You* decide how you react to everything. *You* decide how your character (you) moves through life. When you manage your thoughts, you determine your outcomes.

Thoughts create your emotions, your emotions drive your behaviors, and your behaviors determine your outcomes. Logic would have it, if you figure out how to change your thoughts, you'll set off a life-changing chain reaction.

So, let's talk about Heather's reaction to her mother's comment. Her initial interpretation was that the remark was not only critical, but a signal of personal failure. These thoughts created ashamed and angry feelings inside of her. Now, we're about to get to the second "B": Behavior. If Heather continues with her current interpretation, the "O" (i.e., Outcome) will likely not end in a happy place.

As I'm sure you can predict by now, positive feelings prompt helpful behavior where negative feelings incite unhelpful behavior. Let's explore a few of Heather's potential ABCBO sequences, pending the way she chose to think about the event:

Activating Event (A)	Belief or Thoughts (B) *What Heather thought*	Consequential Emotions (C) *What Heather felt*	Behavior (B) *What Heather did*	Outcome (O)
Mom made a comment about the kids	*Mom criticizing my parenting means I'm a terrible parent.*	Anger, shame	Heather reacts with anger and has an intense argument with her mother.	Heather leaves dinner early and tells her mom not to bother calling anytime soon.
Mom made a comment about the kids	*Mom shouldn't be nosing into business that isn't hers.*	Annoyance	Heather replies to her mother with a passive-aggressive comment.	Heather's mother is offended, feeds into the conflict, and their evening is filled with tension.
Mom made a comment about the kids	*Mom is commenting on how different our parenting styles are.*	Calm, unbothered	Heather accepts the comment, moves on, and pours her mom a glass of wine.	Heather and her family enjoy the evening together.

Outcomes are what we create in our lives through our behavior, which is driven by the feelings we create with our thoughts. Depending upon how Heather chose to receive her mother's comment, the outcomes differed wildly. And we only outlined three potential examples. The options are endless, and they all would trace right back to Heather's thoughts and how she chose to respond to them. What if Heather felt the anger and shame of the first example, and understood what was happening inside her brain? What if she'd been able to name the emotion and examine the thoughts behind it? It's fairly safe to assume she and her mother would still be on speaking terms. If you think about it, Heather's outcome in each potential situation proved her belief to be true. Think about your own ABCBOs—isn't that kind of the way it goes?

Say your boss makes a comment about your work (Activating Event), and you have the thought *I'm terrible at this job* (Belief). This thought creates feelings of anxiety and stress (Consequential Emotions). If left unchecked, you might hyper-focus on this comment and the potential for more feedback (Behavior). Due to this, perhaps you can't focus well enough to improve your performance, which inevitably results in the recurrence of critical feedback you were dreading in the first place (Outcome). In the end, your outcome mirrors and reinforces your reactive, unmonitored thought.

On the other hand, what if you check yourself and choose to react to your supervisor's words by thinking something like, *I have more to learn and I can figure it out and keep at it until I do*. Well, this would probably create confident, empowered feelings, followed by continued efforts to keep showing up, ask questions, and make professional progress. Whether your mental attitude is figure-it-out or I-can't-do-it, it will be directly related to your results.

Let's look at an example from my own life. If you're a person who feels awkward in social situations—especially when you don't know many people—I'm here to say you're not alone, as I'm right there with you. In new social situations my inner monologue was often littered with thoughts like, *Oh my gosh I'm so awkward. Ugh. Why did I even leave my house? People don't even like talking to me anyways.* These thoughts made me feel anxious and uncomfortable (also sweaty), so I often seemed nervous and awkward. This made it so others—all of whom had their own inner monologue—weren't so eager to talk to me. This natural outcome of my ABCBO chain only proved my original thought about people not rushing to seek my company. Fascinating, huh?

Eventually I had to ask myself: *What thought do I want to be thinking about myself? What thought might lead to having a great chat or two when I'm out?*

Spoiler alert: It was time to choose a new adventure.

EXERCISE: ABCBO YOUR DAY

All right. You're familiar with how we begin these drills by now, right?

Whenever you have distressing or uncomfortable feelings (I know, I know—but this is where the change happens!), pay attention to your inner monologue and write it down. After your thoughts are on paper, you are going to build your own personal ABCBO chart.

Activating Event (A)	Belief or Thoughts (B)	Consequential Emotions (C)	Behavior (B)	Outcome (O)

Do this at least once a day for the next week. This is going to give you an entirely different perspective on what's getting in your way, stressing you out, and creating feelings like anger, hurt, and frustration. Something happens to our brains when we see what we're thinking outside of ourselves and we can connect with ourselves in a more objective, less biased way. You might even find yourself immediately thinking about the situation differently.

Activity Pro-Tip: Record your emotion right off the bat. Start your ABCBO chart in the Consequential Emotion column, then head to "A" and describe what happened in neutral terms. Follow with your belief. From there, you will easily identify your resulting behavior and outcome. For some situations, this process will seem simple, but for others it won't be so clear. However, the more you practice, the faster you will be able to connect everything. You're going to start feeling more in charge of your mind and emotions in no time.

Accelerate gently

As you practice, watch for your brain's attempts to make this process stressful. It may be telling you everything has to be clear every time in order for it to be done correctly or it may build the chart up as a big deal. Keep in mind that you're still learning and this shouldn't be an overwhelming task. Breathe and let yourself learn. If you show up, follow the process, and move at whatever pace makes sense for you, you're doing it exactly right.

We're all beginners at everything we try for the first time. It takes a while to get good. The more you do it, the easier it will become. Soon, you'll notice your brain going through this process automatically, even intentionally directing itself toward the thoughts it wants to think to create the feelings it wants to feel.

Developing a strong level of insight and understanding is key to your journey toward a deep level of emotional intelligence. The ability to identify troublesome thoughts and bring conscientious intention to your responses is truly transformational. Gone will be the days of unbridled reactivity. And just by being here and continuously committing to yourself, you have already started on this journey.

Thoughts that come out of nowhere

Before moving on, we must acknowledge the times when emotions run high even though there was no activating event. Thoughts can come out of nowhere and create great anxiety, anger, or sadness (and positive emotions, too!). It's easy to feed into these intense bouts of emotion, especially because even in these times, our feelings are very real. When this happens, your brain may be rummaging through the closet in an attempt to surprise you with what it's used to feeling. Additionally, worry about the future, regrets from the past, and the anxiety of the unpredictable can come out of what seems like nowhere, and can also throw us right off emotionally. However, just like thoughts that have a clear activating event, if we know what to do with thoughts when they show up, we'll be able to work through them.

TAKEAWAYS

- Use the ABCBO model to understand when your thoughts cause feelings, which drive your behaviors, and determine your outcomes.
- Remember to keep your activating event (A) completely neutral; imagine an impartial observer is describing it.
- Breaking down your reactions to situations regularly and changing your thoughts about them (using your ABCBO chart!) will make all the difference in how you feel in and respond to life.

Journal prompt: What beliefs and thoughts create unnecessary problems in my life and how can I begin to change them?

CHAPTER 5

SELF-COMPASSION

Let's take a pause. This is important.

Ready?

Self-compassion is vital. So vital, in fact, that no matter how hard you try, you will never learn to manage your thoughts (and subsequent feelings) without it.

As your thought awareness increases and you pay more attention to your feelings, your brain will have thoughts about those thoughts (meta, right?). Your brain will call on its old buddies Judgment and Criticism to comment on what you automatically think and feel. It will label you as bad, weak, or stupid for thinking or feeling the way you do. It will tell you other people don't struggle with their thoughts and emotions nearly as much as you do. And these meta thoughts might make you feel even more terrible and you'll want to give up.

Don't. You know why? Because having a healthy relationship with yourself is worth the struggle.

Self-compassion is treating yourself like your own best friend and confidante. It's building a relationship with yourself based on trust, respect, acceptance, and understanding. All healthy relationships are built on these principles, and your relationship with yourself is no exception. Every micro moment of what you say to yourself will either erode or elevate this relationship—so I can't overstate the importance of this concept.

We've been talking a lot about our thoughts and feelings, where they come from, and how they affect us. Self-compassion comes in when we decide how to respond when these thoughts and feelings happen, especially the hard ones. We get to decide what our internal monologue says when we're thinking about our thoughts and feelings. We get to decide whether we say things to ourselves that will hurt or heal us.

When difficult thoughts and feelings come up, we don't just have to repress judgment and criticism. We need to call Self-Compassion to the front row and replace thoughts like, *What's wrong with me?? Why can't I just get over this?* with, *I'm struggling right now, and I'm going to be gentle with myself and figure out how to work through it.*

Researcher Dr Kristin Neff, pioneer and international expert on self-compassion, states self-compassion has three components: kindness, mindfulness, and acceptance.

First, kindness. We need to show ourselves kindness and care no matter what we're thinking, feeling, or experiencing. Yes, you may have just yelled at someone and, yes, that was perhaps not the best mode of interaction and, yes, you probably have some thoughts and feelings about it. But will beating yourself up about it a) change it or b) help you in any way? The answer is a resounding "No!" Our feelings create thoughts, and our thoughts drive our behaviors. Sometimes we miss the mark, but we already know shaming and blaming won't get us anywhere. For example, instead of continuing to punish yourself for yelling at your partner earlier that day, intentionally swap self-judgment for language that is healing. Something like, *Yes, I yelled. I am human. I had a hard day and I didn't cope with it in the best way. That one action does not define who I am. It happened, and I am going to apologize and work on taking a deep breath and a step back next time I'm feeling overwhelmed and agitated.*

Second, mindfulness—the principle of allowing ourselves to have any human experience without judging it, getting worked up about it, or allowing it to control us. Although it may seem nebulous, mindfulness is anything but. When you boil it down, mindfulness is simply learning to observe our human experience with neutrality and without getting all caught up in it. Mindfulness creates the space for us to become curious, non-judgmental observers of our human thoughts and emotions. It allows us to realize the deeper truth of being separate from our thoughts and feelings.

Two of my favorite mindfulness mantras are *I am not my thoughts; I am the thinker of my thoughts* and *I am not my feelings; I am the experiencer of my feelings.* Truly embodying mindfulness takes practice, mostly because we have been reacting for our entire lives rather than responding. To respond, you need time to think. Mindfulness gives us that time. To understand, you need to be open. Mindfulness gives us that openness. Once you can observe your experiences with kindness and objectivity, your internal world will never be the same.

Third, and perhaps the most important part of the self-compassion triad, is recognizing and accepting our common humanity. Neff believes we're never alone and we all struggle with being human. Life is messy and complicated for every single one of us. As activist and author Glennon Doyle says, "Life is brutiful—for everyone. About one-half brutal and one-half beautiful which brings us to brutiful. And as long as the beautiful slightly outweighs the brutal, it makes it all worth it." We are all beautiful, messy humans. And when we stop judging or criticizing ourselves for being human beings with complex human feelings, our ability to understand and sort through them becomes so much easier.

EXERCISE: SELF-COMPASSION TOOL

Even once you are a thought-work pro, some thoughts and feelings will be harder to work through than others. Remember not to judge yourself when this happens, as it's just a fact that sometimes life is more or less difficult. Instead of judgment, you're going to practice a simple exercise designed to keep you from judging yourself during these times. Feelings and thoughts need to be heard whether they're good or bad, right or wrong, helpful or unhelpful, healthy or unhealthy. And you're going to accept any given feeling or thought with a simple sentence:

**It's understandable that I'm feeling/thinking ....
because ....**

Here are some examples from my own repertoire:

- It's understandable that I'm feeling *anxious about this process* because *it's new and my brain is not sure what to do in every situation.*
- It's understandable that *my mind was spinning about whether people were judging me in that meeting/party/activity* because *I want people to think well of me.*
- It's understandable that I'm feeling *worried about saying no to that invitation* because *I don't want to upset anyone.*

When we take the time to listen to and acknowledge our difficult feelings, our brains are far less likely to push back and resist. When we create space for all of our thoughts, compassionately and mindfully, we're less likely to feel stuck and give up on ourselves.

Acknowledge your thoughts and let them feel heard. Be understanding of yourself. Not only will you feel calmer, you'll also have better access to your rational brain. And when you and your rational brain are on friendly terms, you'll get more practice with productive and healthy thoughts, which is why you're here in the first place.

TAKEAWAYS

- Be kind to yourself and try to avoid judging or criticizing yourself for unhelpful or destructive thoughts.
- Be mindful and allow yourself to have your thoughts without getting drawn in; become an observer of life not a reactor to it.
- Remember that everyone has these self-defeating thoughts at times. You are not alone.

Journal prompt: How can I be kinder to myself and offer self-compassion when I'm struggling with my thoughts?

PART TWO
BECOME THE DRIVER OF YOUR OWN EMOTIONS

Now that you're in the know about the lengths to which your brain will go to avoid difficult emotions via food, substances, defensiveness, blaming, mindless social-media scrolling, and various other modes of emotionally motivated behavior, we're going to dig even deeper into it.

In the end, our reactivity makes us feel worse in the long run and doesn't bring us the outcomes we desire. Remember Heather's holiday argument with her mother? All this turmoil because we don't know how to sit with and truly understand our uncomfortable feelings. Instead of becoming genuinely curious about ourselves, we run away screaming from emotional discomfort.

You also know this is at least partially because many of us were never taught or encouraged to feel. We all remember those common adult reactions to our emotions. Things like, "Don't get upset!", "Okay, okay. Get over it," and, my favorite, "Just let it go!" And now that you're the adult, you think things like, *I'm a grown-up and I should be able to manage my emotions*, or, *What's wrong with me?* and, *Why do I feel so emotionally out of control?* and, *Why can't I get it together?*

I know I felt this way for the first 30+ years of my life. If you haven't picked up on it by now, despite the counselling degree, I was a bit of an emotional mess myself. It wasn't with every situation or all the time, but it was more than what I thought was my fair share. Feelings of jealousy, hurt, and offense were all too common for me. I took interactions personally more often than I wouldn't. And, to top it off, I'd attempt to force myself out of these feelings, telling myself I was being stupid and immature for having them.

Knowing what I know now, it wasn't the best strategy; but at the time, it seemed like my only option. Even though criticizing myself for my feelings never actually made me feel better, I thought if I strong-armed myself into being confident and secure, I would be. Perhaps predictably, this method didn't work.

Thankfully, there are far better options than trying to make yourself feel better by telling yourself how bad you are. Let's rev her up, shall we?

CHAPTER 6
SHAME AND SELF-WORTH

Shame.

Over my years of therapeutic practice, I've become what some may think is too comfortable with talking openly about shame. In my defense, though, shame is as normal as making plans for the future. We all have at least some. But unlike our much-anticipated summer vacation, we don't really want to talk about it because, well... shame. But the less we talk about it, the worse it gets. So we're not going to let it swallow us whole today; we're going to bring it right out in the open and look at it bravely.

Shame sits inside your brain and whispers lies to your subconscious about what makes you a fundamentally unworthy human being. Shame says, "You're less valuable, less lovable, less capable, less competent, or less significant than everyone else." And sometimes Shame ever so persistently convinces us we need to change the core of who we are in order to achieve "good enough" status.

In her book, *Daring Greatly*, Brené Brown wrote, "Shame is the intensely painful feeling or experience of believing that we are flawed and therefore unworthy of love and belonging—something we've experienced, done, or failed to do makes us unworthy of connection [with both ourselves and others]."

In our bodies, the shame often feels like a hot, tense sensation flooding us from head to toe. It may also show up as tunnel vision, tingling in the armpits, a lump in the throat, or a flip-flopping stomach. Shame can show up in the sneakiest ways, coming out of nowhere to crush us without warning—sometimes from surprising sources.

For example, when I look at the self-help industry, I see many unintentional trends toward self-shaming. This perhaps occurs most frequently with the commonly posed question, "Who do you want to become?" While this sounds inspirational and motivational on the surface, the underlying message is, "Who you are now is not good enough, and you need to become someone or something else in order to make the mark."

But your healing and growth should never be about becoming *someone else*. It should be focused on becoming your authentic self. The self who is hidden under shame, pain, fear, and defensiveness. This process is not about becoming someone else. It's about becoming more you than you've ever been. While growth may involve changing how you show up, express yourself, and approach your life, who you are has always been and will always be perfectly imperfect. Who you are doesn't need changing; it simply needs revealing.

EXERCISE: WHAT DOES SHAME FEEL LIKE IN MY BODY?

Think about all the exercises you worked through in Part One. Now you're going to home in on one specific feeling instead of just your feelings in general. The next time you feel shame, I want you to STOP and PAY ATTENTION to how this emotion feels in your body. Is it hotness in your head, tightness in your chest, tingling in your armpits? Something else? Write down in detail where and how it shows up. You got this.

Where does shame come from?

Shame comes from the intersection of childhood experiences and cultural messaging. Throughout history, shame has been used to keep people in line. In fact, "shameful exposure" was a popular tactic in the 19th century and before—think stockades. These days, we aren't upholding the law because of a fear of a public shaming ceremony. However, we are certainly living our lives to avoid our deep shame and prove our worthiness at all costs. Today, it seems mainstream capitalist culture paves the way for shame by telling us we need to *have* more, *be* more, and *do* more before we can be good enough. Any messaging we experienced that is rooted in the ideology that something outside of ourselves proves our worthiness lays the foundation for shame. I'm not just talking about advertisements.

Remember, at any given moment, we hold within us narratives we were told and taught about ourselves, who we are, who we should be, who we aren't, who our parents wanted us to be, why we don't measure up, and why we aren't good enough. Perhaps the adults in your life openly or covertly shamed you by wondering aloud, "Why am I raising such a troublemaker?" or, "What's wrong with you?" or, "Why can't you be more like [insert kid who always did everything right here]?" As children we instinctively trust our parents, whether or not that trust is earned. Children are also more self-focused and egocentric than adults, so they end up thinking abuse or mistreatment is their own fault. A child's brain cannot comprehend that adult mistreatment and name-calling has nothing to do with them— it was really just about the grown-ups in your life not being able to manage their own minds and emotions, and then taking it out on you. When, as children, we internalize criticisms, comparisons, and labels, our brains absorb these messages and create negative beliefs that often follow us into adulthood. And so here we are.

Our personal shames haunt us and affect the way we interact with our world. We are susceptible to predatory companies who are willing to bet the odds that many people can be sold on products based on avoiding or diminishing shame. In other words, the media uses our shame against us for its gain. *You need this eye cream because your naturally aging skin isn't good enough* or, *If you don't have as much money as your brother/friend/neighbor you have fundamentally failed.* We are constantly bombarded with messaging reminding us that who we are doesn't quite measure up.

This, paired with the cultural and social messaging, leaves us feeling like we must have missed the lesson when we were taught how to be normal, well-functioning human beings who didn't constantly question whether or not they were good enough. It's like everybody else got the memo and we were left out of it somehow. And so, we walk around the world feeling like there's something wrong with us—wondering why we feel lonely and utterly unworthy of love. We conclude there's something fundamentally unlovable and inferior about us, because everyone else got the script on how to be normal, perfect, and whole, while we were left with scraps of paper resulting in our being weird, flawed, and broken.

Personally, though, I think weird, flawed, and broken is beautiful because weird, flawed, and broken is real. And hey, news flash: "Normal" doesn't even exist other than the illusion of it on the surface.

Our shame stories

Because we are human, and humans are storytellers, when we experience shame-inducing situations, we create stories about ourselves based on our experiences. Unfortunately, these stories often revolve around our core beliefs about ourselves and our self-worth, or lack thereof.

Shame is an expert at adding a personal twist to our experiences:

Shame says, "I AM unlovable," instead of, "I felt unloved."

Shame says, "I AM a reject," instead of, "That person chose someone else."

Shame says, "I AM a mistake," instead of, "I made a mistake."

Shame says, "I AM a failure," instead of, "I experienced a failure."

Shame says, "I AM not good enough," instead of, "I could have done better."

Thanks, Shame—you're a gem.

EXERCISE: TAKE AWAY YOUR "SHAME TRIGGER"

Make a list of the three most common thoughts you have that bring up feelings of shame. They could be about your worth, your achievements, your lovability, or anything else. Maybe your shame trigger is *I'm not good enough* or *I'm not lovable*. We all have a shame trigger (or several) that kicks us when we're already feeling down. Think of up to three, and then we're going to work through them.

Write them on a piece of paper and then use your neutralizing skills to reduce the emotional charge of each statement. As we know, this will start to decrease the intensity. For example, replace *I don't have what it takes* with *I'm struggling to believe in myself right now* or, *This isn't as easy as I thought it would be*. Another example could be shifting *I'm a failure* to *I didn't get the outcome I wanted*. This will probably be difficult at first, so take your time. You've been thinking these shame scripts for a long time, so creating counteractive, shame-challenging statements isn't going to be easy.

Hint: You'll know you've been successful with this exercise when your shame reaction transitions from fully overtaking your brain and body, to manageable feelings of disappointment, hurt, or another less visceral emotion.

Women and shame

In recent years, I've worked with an influx of women in the 25–45-year-old range who are specifically struggling with body-image issues and a hateful view of their physical appearance. There's an immense, complicated history of the patriarchy using women's bodies as a self-destructive weapon. Our society abides by fabricated beauty standards for women to aspire to, which essentially teaches women to hate their bodies, faces, hair, etc., pushing them toward endless products and programs to make them feel more worthy. From childhood, women receive messages emphasizing their appearance over so many other things, which keeps them in a place of inferiority.

Undoing this issue requires immense, deep thought work. But for now, whether you identify as a guy, a gal, or non-binary pal, I want you to read this and know it to be true: Neither the size nor the shape of your human body is an objectively moral issue. What your body looks like is not an indication of whether you're good, bad, superior, or inferior. What you eat or don't eat is not a measure of your worth; your food choices do not make you worse than or better than. Your human body has never been and will never be a part of you that is inherently shameful.

You weren't born to hate your body; you were taught to shame it.

Cultivating shame

As if it weren't enough, shame also breeds trouble in relationships. When we're struggling with shame, we unconsciously rely on how others treat us to indicate how worthy we are of love. Have you ever secretly thought to yourself that if your partner or best friend truly loved you, they'd go out of their way to plan a big birthday bash for you? After all, you've been hinting at it for months and you *always* go way above and beyond for them. You reason that if they truly love you, they'd want to do something extra special for your birthday. Then when they take you for a lackluster dinner at your regular restaurant, you're angry, disappointed, and hurt.

When I think about shame spirals, I always time-hop to a period in my life when making plans with a certain group of friends was almost sure to send me into a tailspin of emotional self-abuse. In my mind, it appeared I was always the one to initiate plans and demonstrate effort to keep our group friendships alive. However, since it felt like I was the only one making an effort, when I'd reach out to plan something, my brain would whirl into inner dialogue like, *Why don't they care to hang out with me the same way I do with them? Do they not value, or even like me as much as I thought they did? Maybe they've finally realized how extra I can be and they're over it... and me reaching out is just confirming this. Ugh, I'm just a reject. I don't even belong and probably never will.*

Whoa, right? I know. But this is reality—this is what we do to ourselves when others' actions (or our perception of them) are a primary measure of our own self-worth. This is also exactly why we really need to take a step back, understand our expectations vs. reality, and openly reflect on the role shame plays in our lives.

Your turn. Think about a time when something didn't go the way you expected it to and, in that moment, it meant something about who you inherently are. We all do it, so where do we go from here?

Self-acceptance

The difference between those who frequently struggle with shame and those who seem to more easily float above it really starts with our individual beliefs about our inherent worthiness. That's it. The seemingly shame-less have arrived at the belief that they are worthy because they were born; they don't have to do anything to prove or earn it.

I truly used to believe that I felt so much more shame than other people because I inherently had more imperfections to be ashamed of, but I've slowly come to grips with the fact that we all have shame, and we can talk about it openly, name it, and accept it; there is no reason to be threatened by it. The very nature of shame is isolating, so when we can shine a light on it and normalize it, it sort of dissipates.

You see, those who live without shame have made peace with their imperfections and let themselves live as perfectly imperfect beings. They've let go of trying to be who they should be and have decided to be who they are. They know they don't have it all together because, well, they are human, so of course they don't. That's all it takes—the courage to let yourself be imperfect. This journey we are on isn't about trying to be perfect so we don't have to feel shame; it's about accepting ourselves where we are, and loving ourselves every step of the way. We're going to look at the importance of a strong sense of self-love and belonging in Chapter 13. Until then, be gentle with yourself, okay?

TAKEAWAYS

- Shame stems from a lack of self-worth and beliefs that you're not worthy of acceptance, love, or success.
- The healing work is about changing *how* you are, not *who* you are. You are already enough.
- Recognize when shame triggers unhealthy expectations of others and yourself.
- The most profound thing we can do is accept, love, appreciate, and recognize ourselves for the perfectly imperfect beings that we are.

Journal prompt: How would my life change if I could love and accept myself no matter what, imperfections and all?

CHAPTER 7
ANXIETY AND STRESS

Like any human emotion, anxiety is not right or wrong, good or bad. We all feel anxious sometimes. However, anxiety becomes a problem when it comes on long and strong; and it can also wreak havoc if it's always humming under the surface, causing you to feel a little uneasy and on edge no matter the circumstance.

Chances are, if you're resonating with the concepts in this book, Anxiety, like Shame, is an old frenemy of yours. As we do, let's take a closer look at what anxiety is all about.

For the most part, anxiety is created by our thoughts just like any other emotion. In *Mind Over Mood*, Drs Dennis Greenberger and Christine Padesky dive into the two common types of anxious people: *worriers* and *perfectionists*.

The Worriers
Unsurprisingly, worriers worry. But it's not your regular old worrying-for-a-reason. Worriers worry about little things and big things. They fret over real possibilities and highly-unlikely-to-come-about freak accidents. They agonize over the unexpected, the terrible, and the potential. They worry about being too late, arriving too early, running out of supplies, overbuying, leaving their old job, starting their new job, what will happen when they travel, and what they'll do if the world comes to an end. This is not your mother's anxiety (or maybe it is). Worriers have

a deep, constant feeling that something is about to go wrong and calamity is lurking right around the corner.

In their defense, their worrying is based in an element of self-preservation. Often, worriers believe their anxiety prevents bad things from happening, since the result of their worry is over-planning, over-preparing, and over-caution. This could be, in part, somewhat accurate. (But it's still not helpful for their mental and emotional state.)

The worrier's subconscious brain also believes terrible things only happen when it's least expected; hence, if they can anticipate all terrible things, they won't happen. Technically, if you look at their lives from this perspective, most, if not all, of the awful things they've lost sleep over haven't actually happened. Their brains think it must be working; but it's a far-reaching correlation at best. Really, they're in a cyclical thought–feeling routine that's saving no one, especially themselves.

The Perfectionists

Perfectionists, on the other hand, are embroiled in a whole other kind of anxiety. Often, perfectionistic brains believe their internal and external worlds must be impeccable and their job is to make everyone around them happy and comfortable. They put tremendous pressure on themselves to appear to "have it together" and do everything exactly right. This mindset is essentially a worthiness hustle. *If I just achieve/do/please/perfect/perform more... then I won't have to feel anxious. I'll finally feel good about myself.*

Perfectionists struggle with overcommitting, setting healthy boundaries (which we'll cover more in Chapter 17), and trying to be everything to everyone; they want to feel needed and necessary, which isn't bad in itself. However, perfectionistic anxiety is propelled through a deep fear of inherent unworthiness, and they tend to believe people won't love them if they're not perfect.

This too-high level of expectations causes perfectionists to stall on dreams, goals, and taking action. The agony of contemplating what it may mean if they fail or make a mistake can be paralyzing. Not only does this type of anxiety take an emotional toll, it literally holds many people back from doing the work to uncover their most authentic self.

The perfectionist is also known for being productive and getting a lot done, but they do so while swimming exhaustedly up a stream of self-doubt and "I just need to do a little more" the entire way. If, right now, you're thinking to yourself, *No, Julia, I'm not a perfectionist because I already know nothing I ever do is good enough.* Well, my friend, I hate to tell you this, but that is the perfectionist's anthem. Perfectionists *never* think they are perfect, but always have the perfect version of themselves as their ultimate, "I will finally be worthy enough when I am" goalpost.

EXERCISE: CREATE YOUR GROUNDING THOUGHTS

Below you'll find a bank of sentences you can use to ground yourself when you notice worried, anxious, or stressed feelings are starting to permeate your mind. When this happens, pick two or three of the lines and repeat them to yourself. They'll serve as healthy reminders to be more present, accepting, and anchored. When you find a few that work for you, write them down and carry them with you. A slip of paper in your pocket, a sticky note on your mirror, or the home screen of your phone are perfect places to keep them. When you find yourself intentionally thinking them because they make you feel better, consider it progress.

19 Grounding Thoughts

1. I have coped with similar situations and have been fine.

2. I must find a path through, but I don't have to do it perfectly.
3. I don't have to do everything myself; I can ask for help.
4. This is only going to last a little while longer. I can handle it.
5. This struggle is temporary.
6. Anxiety is uncomfortable but it won't kill me.
7. Worrying doesn't change anything; it only stresses me and wastes my time.
8. I don't have to do everything right; sometimes good enough is good enough.
9. If I avoid things, my anxiety will get worse. If I act even though I'm scared, I will grow.
10. A little anxiety is normal.
11. Things don't have to go my way for me to be okay.
12. I can do hard things. I have before and I can again.
13. Right now, in this moment, I am okay.
14. This worry will be irrelevant this time next week or next month.
15. This too shall pass.
16. I am safe right now.
17. I am good enough even when I don't do everything others expect me to do.
18. This feeling is just a physical sensation. It will pass.
19. My thoughts are creating my discomfort.

The illusion of control

Control and the attempts to achieve it are at the heart of anxiety and stress. Anxiety is an iteration of fear. It manifests through the feelings brought on by a lack of control and uncertainty. Our brains tell us the way to decrease our anxiety is to be (or think we are) more in control. If we can be absolutely sure of what's happening and what's going to happen, then there's nothing to fear. At least your buddy Anxiety certainly likes you to think so.

Trying to control the countless aspects of your life is like playing a game of whack-a-mole. The second you whack the last mole and you think all is well, another mole pops up. Then another. Then three more. You'll never relax, and you'll be whacking till kingdom comes. There is no end, no solution, and no feasible goal—just a seemingly pointless game that's not nearly as fun as you remember it to be.

Have you ever noticed when you're feeling stressed about being out of control with the bigger things in your life (i.e. your finances, your relationship, your job stress), you work to over-control smaller things that have nothing to do with the real origin of the stress? For me, it's my house. When I'm feeling overwhelmed or out of control in my life, I overcompensate by cleaning anything and everything within the confines of my home with unmatched desperation. Perhaps for you it's overplanning, creating a new color-code system for your calendar, or double- and triple-checking everything you do.

So now it's time I let you in on a little secret. *Control doesn't exist.* It's an illusion; full control is not actually achievable. Ever. At all. Just like with whack-a-mole, we can achieve a hint of control for a moment, but no sooner do we think we finally have it than up pops the next mole. The more we desperately strive for control, the more out of reach it becomes.

EXERCISE: HOW TO UNPACK UNHELPFUL OR HIGH EXPECTATIONS

If you're feeling defeated at the revelation that control doesn't exist, don't quit on me yet. There's a difference between being in control and being in charge. Here is where we are going to unpack the unhelpful expectations you have for yourself so you'll be able to take charge of your mind and emotions when you're feeling like the game of whack-a-mole will never end.

Take a few minutes to ponder the following:

• What unhelpful expectations do you have for yourself that lead to feelings of frustration and self-defeat?

- Who else in your life do you hold to high expectations?
- How often do you feel like you're failing at being a good enough parent, partner, employee, boss, or friend?
- How do you talk to yourself when you don't meet the expectation you've set for yourself? Are you kind or unkind? Are you forgiving or hardened?
- Do the expectations you have for yourself make you a better person? If so, how? If not, how do you feel at the end of most days?

Have you ever thought about where the expectations you have for yourself come from? Think about it. Yep, that's right—they are literally made up. There's no divine or written rule proclaiming how much you must give, do, sacrifice, achieve, or accomplish in a day to tick all the "good enough" boxes. Your unachievable standards are, in fact, arbitrary, and so is the mental beating you give yourself when you don't meet them.

The solution? Set new standards you can achieve and fulfill them. Commit to less, take on less, agree to less and, for heaven's sake, please beat yourself up less. And while we're here, let's talk about how this also applies to the unfair expectations we have for not only ourselves, but for others.

I said it. Others. You may be thinking, *No, Julia, I'm WAY harder on myself than I am on others.* In which case, I have a challenge for you. Make a mental (or physical) list of the people you are currently harboring resentment toward for some reason or another. Who has disappointed you recently? These feelings, at their core, are most likely connected to the fact that your expectations of that person or relationship haven't been met.

For a long time, I believed my unrealistic expectations extended to myself only. A long-time student of being hard on myself, I believed I was failing at most things. Guilty for not doing enough for my family, not being home enough with my kids, not serving enough for my online community, I was riddled with can't-stop-won't-stop perfectionistic anxiety and

I thought that was where it ended. But then, one day as I was staring at my phone, frustrated with yet another person in my life who had disappointed me, I realized how much resentment I was harboring toward others due to nothing other than the expectations I had of them. It was then I realized it was time for me to let all of it go.

And since there is no time like the present, let's dive in. Yes, I'm serious. We're doing this now!

Take a minute to think about every expectation you have for yourself; focus on the ones you never seem to meet. Once you have that list in mind, take another minute to imagine what it would be like to lower those expectations so you can actually achieve them. As you do this, you may feel triggered by the very notion of lowering expectations. I get it. Here's the thing though: yet another thing we've been culturally shaped to do is to create sky-high expectations for ourselves that are often designed to be impossible to hit. Also, if you're honest with yourself, they're also moving targets. There is nothing wrong with lowering your expectations. The saying "Go big or go home" is not all that helpful or all that sustainable. So how about we change it to "Go small to moderate and make it doable and sustainable." Not quite as sexy, but oh so much more helpful.

Next, think about any resentments you're carrying with you about the people in your life. Visualize removing any and all the expectations you have for others that they cannot meet (because they likely don't even know about them). Then do it. Take them down. Let them go. Create new, realistic, flexible ones for both yourself and others.

Feel lighter yet?

Trust

So, if neither control nor high expectations is the solution to make you feel calmer, grounded, and at peace, what will? The reality is rooted to another seemingly basic piece of grace we have to give ourselves. It's something so simple that we often give it to others and forget altogether that we deserve it too.

Trust.

The antidote to anxiety is trust. Trust that no matter what happens, you will figure it out. Trust that you can work with whatever life throws at you. Trust in yourself to cope through hard things. Trust that even when you're not okay, you will figure out a way to get back to okay. Trust that you will catch yourself instead of kick yourself when you fall. Besides, we all fall in life.

Trust is not throwing caution to the wind and being irresponsible, by the way. Trust is finding a balance between responsibility, rationality, and the inverse. If you believe something terrible will happen and you won't be able to cope, you're going to feel vulnerable and spin out of control. When you trust that you can deal with most situations, anxiety has nowhere to go. Trust isn't planning your escape route to the nth degree; it's believing your inner strength will provide.

What does anxiety feel like in the body?

While anxiety almost always begins with your thoughts—like every other emotion—it can manifest itself in numerous physical ways. We've talked briefly about some of the physiological sensations of anxiety, but let's review. Anxiety can show up as a racing heart, shallow breath, tight throat, heaviness in your chest, seeing spots, dizziness, clammy hands, sweating, or that flip-flopping gut. How does anxiety feel to you? Taking the time to understand your physiological response of anxiety is perhaps one of the most helpful things you can do for yourself. Not only will learning this assist you to dial down your anxiety in the moment, but it will also help you understand its source(s). When you know your triggers, you can properly and preemptively manage them. Keep reflecting.

Tuning into your rational mind

As you know, when you're amped up on anxiety, your brain is in survival mode and reacts as such. Your emotional brain is in the driver's seat while your rational brain heads right to the back of the bus. When you aren't amped up, you're able to think of practical solutions to the problem at hand, right? But when you're overwhelmed with a flood of emotion pumping through your body, it's way harder to do so.

When you feel this happen, taking the edge off your anxiety is key. Bringing yourself to a calmer, more grounded state will help your emotional brain take the backseat and allow your rational brain to sit in the driver's seat. The first step is to reduce the physical experience of your anxiety. There's no way to immediately turn it off, but you can diffuse your internal tension through engaging your body and mind in alternate ways.

1. *Deep breaths*
This one's quick and simple. More oxygen to the brain increases blood flow and gets your inner workings going. When you're feeling stressed and anxious, everything becomes tense without you knowing it. With deep breaths you can reach a natural state of more calm. When employing this strategy, take deep belly breaths and focus on the exhale. As you push out the air, imagine you are pushing out your stress and tension. **Pro-Tip:** If you start to feel light-headed, you may be pushing too hard. Keep going but focus on a more natural out-breath.

Often, you'll start to feel calmer after only a couple of breaths. When you feel this physical grounding, you'll have renewed access to your rational mind. And when you have that, you'll be much better equipped to work through whatever is triggering your anxiety—something you can't do when the emotional center of your brain thinks it needs to fight for its life.

If nothing else, start with breath when you are facing a difficult emotion. It's the first step to your rational mind and is sure to serve you well.

2. *Take a walk*
Another way to diffuse tension and emotion is to take a walk. I'm not talking about a two-hour HIIT workout at the gym (although that's fine if you have time); a trot around the neighborhood will do. Taking a quick walk is another way to get increased oxygen and blood flow circulating in your brain and body. When we move our bodies, naturally happy and anxiety-calming chemicals called endorphins are released.

I remember when I was writing my thesis for grad school, there were several nights when I thought I was at the end of my tether. I wanted to chuck my computer out of our second-story apartment window because I was so frustrated with the slow and painful progress I was making on the 120-page research paper I'd been working on for a year. Thankfully, my husband knew me well enough to (firmly, but lovingly) say, "Just put your runners on and get out of here."

After a few stress-fueled protests, he'd inevitably win, and out the door I'd go. Without fail, every time I took a 10-minute jaunt through the neighbourhood, I would walk back in the door saying, "Okay, I'm better, let's do this." And then I would get back to cranking out the pages. **Pro-Tip**: To make this emotional reset even more effective, call a (super-supportive) friend while you're walking. Talking out what and how you're feeling is a powerful thing—just make sure you return the favor so your friends don't feel like they are your emotional dumping ground.

3. *Simple hand exercise*
A mindfulness exercise you can do as a gentle form of self-hypnosis is what's known as the "Following Hand Movement." Slightly cup your hand, keeping your four fingers together.

Rub the tip of your thumb slowly back and forth across your fingertips while you watch the movement. Observe your thumb as it moves along the bumps your fingers make. Notice everything about what it feels like—the ridges, the texture, the color of your skin. This simple grounding exercise gets you out of your head and connects you with your body, your senses, and the present moment. Time yourself for 30–60 seconds. Your brain will automatically calm as it grounds itself and discontinues the thought, worry, fear and anxiety spirals you may be experiencing.

4. *Calm your brain*
Finally—and this is my favorite because it's kind of silly—try hanging upside down! A chin-up bar or the parallel bars are perfect for this. You can also simulate this by standing with your feet hip-width apart and folding over so your head hangs between your legs. It may sound like a funny trick but going upside down can have a major impact on your emotional state. It brings extra blood and oxygen to your brain, which has a natural calming effect. When you hang like this for a minute or two, you'll find that you feel more relaxed, have a clearer head, and feel ready for what lies ahead. **Pro-Tip**: Don't forget to come right side up slowly in case of light-headedness.

Get comfortable with being uncomfortable

Trying to avoid anxiety-provoking situations may seem like the smart thing to do every time you feel that anxious twinge in your belly, but, however tempting, it doesn't help long-term. It just delays the inevitable. Although your primitive brain likes nothing more than to stay safe, comfortable, and conserve energy, it's pretty hard to progress and grow if you keep isolating yourself out of avoidance of discomfort.

Pushing yourself to cope with new and (mild to moderately) anxiety-inducing situations on a regular basis will help to rework parts of your brain. It may not feel great, but when you do this, you're showing your brain that you can handle challenges without harm befalling you. The danger signals your brain is sending will die down as it realizes the threat it's feeling isn't nearly as imminent as it thinks it is, and starting your side hustle, giving a presentation at work, or speaking up about something that's important to you isn't going to kill you.

Be mindful of how stressful the anxious-thought-provoking situation is as you practice. Too much all at once may not be enough time for your brain to adapt and could make it worse. For example, you may not want to invest millions into a jewelry business right off the bat, but an Etsy shop might be a good place to start. If you feel uncomfortable speaking in public, don't go right to leading the next company-wide in-service, but perhaps start by volunteering to lead the next small team meeting. Get comfortable with being uncomfortable one small step at a time.

Challenging ourselves to work through uncomfortable experiences while acknowledging that we are not fully in control signals to your brain that you can handle what life gives you. The South African psychiatrist Joseph Wolpe coined this process as "systematic desensitization." When you do this, you are desensitizing yourself to the things you fear most—in a systematized way.

Acknowledging your anxiety, getting curious about it, and being with it is a hard, but necessary, step in the process of becoming the driver of your own life. There's no need to shame or criticize yourself for being a normal human being who isn't perfectly calm all the time, and learning to be with discomfort is the primary means to build a rich, rewarding, and colorful life. There will be times when this is easier said than done, but doing hard things is worth it because that's how you get unstuck.

As you prove to yourself that you can stretch bit by little bit, you're creating a beautiful feedback loop for yourself, thereby making it easier to trust yourself with the roadblock and challenges you face down the road.

TAKEAWAYS

- Anxiety and stress often stem from the brain's outdated need to "belong" and "fit in."
- Control is an illusion.
- Trusting in yourself and your ability to face challenges is the antidote to stress and anxiety.
- Stop avoiding anxiety-provoking situations and experiences; instead face them one step at a time.

Journal prompt: In which areas of my life can I step into discomfort as an opportunity to learn, grow, and experience?

CHAPTER 8
DEMOTIVATION AND BEING STUCK

Whether you're going back to school, making a career change, getting through the gigantic laundry pile, starting a side business, finishing that book you started six months ago, building in those 30 movement minutes daily, or re-entering the dating world after a break-up, motivation is a tricky beast. How do you start something and then keep going strong? How do you find the motivation and energy to begin, maintain, and not give up when shit gets real, and the excitement of getting to your goal is tarnished by the hours of mundane, often repetitive work required to get there?

I used to think of consistently motivated, productive people as super humans who have leveled up in ways I could only imagine. You know those people. The ones who complete their to-do lists, make a lot of promises, and then follow through on all of their commitments, and always seem to move with purpose. I thought they had a gene I didn't, and I was just one of the unfortunate ones who got the spurts-of-motivation-followed-by-an-array-of-self-doubt-and-serious-consideration-of-avoiding-it-all gene instead.

Turns out, I was wrong. These leveled-up people aren't born this way and they don't naturally wake up motivated and buzzing with excitement. They also occasionally wake up with the burning desire to hit the snooze button for the next four hours. They do have a secret, though. Wanna hear it? They don't wait to *become* motivated; they *make* themselves motivated.

Consistent people don't buy into the lie that motivation must precede work. They move past their primitive brain pitching every excuse in the book and they just get started. They choose their thoughts intentionally to create feelings to drive their action and get their desired results. In other words, they focus on what they want, ignore the part of their brain that wants to conserve energy in case of a natural disaster, and do what they need to do. People who get shit done have relentless excuse-making brains encouraging them to stay on the couch and binge Netflix like you and me. They've just learned to redirect their thoughts to the alternate: *I'm not going to get what I want by sitting here doing nothing, so I may as well get my butt in gear and get going instead.*

I was sort of hoping there would be a magic motivation elixir, too (the closest I ever got was Red Bull, but I hear too much of that can mess you up, so that's out). If I burst your bubble, I'll make up for it by sharing the upside: If other people with brains just like yours learn to redirect their thoughts, so can you.

Stuck in our heads

Human brains are wired to be lazy *and* wired for growth. It's a contradiction, but what about being human isn't? You already know the primitive part of your brain wants you to do as little as possible to conserve energy in case your camp gets raided by a pride of hungry lions. On the other hand (or brain), the more sophisticated, highly developed part of your brain wants more than to just be alive. This part of your brain wants meaning, purpose, creativity, and a sense of love and belonging; it lights up when you learn, grow, experience, create, connect, and contribute—pushing you toward a richer and more rewarding existence.

If you're not managing your mind, when your desire for creative pursuits and personal growth gets you started, your initial resolve wears off after a time. It's as if your primitive brain shows up with lame excuses and your evolved brain hasn't quite figured out how to consistently call the bluff yet. Sound familiar?

When this happens, it's like you're driving your bus with one foot on the gas and the other on the brake. We're expending energy to get going but keep stalling out, and don't get far at all.

So, let's get your foot off the brake.

Get out of your head and into your life

First things first: stop listening to your feelings. There. Yes, I said it. This may seem like a contradiction to the first several chapters and exercises in this book, but let me explain. There's a difference between processing your feelings to gain understanding, and making your feelings the basis of your decision-making (which humans do—all the time). When I say stop listening to your feelings, I mean it's time to recognize that your feelings are not always an accurate interpretation of your environment and experience. Which, by the way, *is* what you've been learning to do.

You see, sometimes your feelings lie to you and don't have your best interests at heart. And since most of your feelings come from thoughts—which are subjective stories based on your perceptions—when your feelings say you're not in the mood to do, grow, make, be, etc., how can you possibly take their word for it? So, if you're always asking yourself if you *feel* like pounding out that 52-page proposal or chilling on the couch, nine times out of ten, your feelings would have you on the sofa scrolling through your phone.

What do you do with that? You change the question. Instead of giving your feelings the final say by asking yourself what you *feel* like doing, you're going to ask yourself something else entirely: "What is in my best interest?" See how this tweak changes everything? It's far more difficult for your brain to tell you to sit and scroll when you ask it like this because, well, when is scrolling ever in your best interest? And if you're honest with yourself about what the answer to the new question is— the things that will move you forward, make you healthier, and get you a step closer to achieving your goals and dreams is going to win every time.

Find your why

Once you get out of your feelings, it's important to regularly connect with all the reasons you're trying to do x, y, or z. Why does x matter do you? Why is y your thing? Why do you want to do z? What are all these things going to change for you and your life?

To change your relationship with your goals—especially ones you're stuck on—is to move them off your traditional to-do list and incorporate them into your life using an emotional connection. This makes reaching your goals about "being" rather than "doing." They are more than tasks; they are more than the minutiae of the day-to-day.

Maybe you're looking to make changes in your career. Don't just have this goal be represented by a to-do bullet point like, *Apply for 5 jobs this week*. Give it meaning. Think about why you are looking for something new. Perhaps you want to wake up excited about doing something important in the world. Maybe you need a greater sense of purpose. Look beyond the bullet and carve out time in your schedule for *Connecting with organizations that serve a purpose where I can be an asset*.

When it comes to motivation, asking yourself *Why?* is the first thing you should do after you stop giving your feelings so much decision-making sway. Why do you want to move your body every day? Why do you want to nail the proposal? Why do you want to date again? Why do you want to start a business? Why do you want to learn how to drive your own darn bus? The deeper and more meaningful your why, the easier it will be to take action.

Time for some real talk. I do not wake up motivated every day. No matter how long I've been driving my own bus, I do not jump out of bed singing, "Hello, beautiful day! Let's seize you!" No. I'm the personification of no-talkie-before-coffee. No matter how I'm feeling on any given day, the one thing that keeps me moving forward is asking myself, "Why am I doing this, and what will I do if I don't? What's the alternative?" If I don't reply to my emails, complete my clerical tasks that need to be addressed, or create content for my next YouTube video series, what will I do instead? What's the alternative if I give up and say I don't feel like it? Do I want to go back to a small, dark, windowless office to work at a job that doesn't feed my soul?

And then I get my second cup of coffee.

This isn't to say you will be motivated to achieve every distant goal you ever have. If you start working on a goal and realize the alternative is what you actually want to be doing—great! Discernment is what finding your why is all about. If something isn't important to you, it's not getting you where you want to go, it drains you, and you have the means and ability to stop doing it, stop! Otherwise, stop Googling political parody videos, pause Netflix, close Instagram, and get to it.

Get up and dance

Movement lights us up. When you change the state of your body, you change the state of your mind. We've been mostly focused on how to use your thoughts to spur you into action, but using your body to get you into a better state of mind is an effective little tool, too.

I batch-record my YouTube videos on a set day every month. If I wake up with a case of the "blahs" on my recording day, the last thing I often feel like doing is being engaging, interesting, and informative on camera. But I have a backup plan.

"Alexa, play pump-up music."

Then Alexa, serotonin (i.e. happy chemicals released by my brain), and I have a solid kitchen dance party, and I'm good to go. Of course, dancing may not work for you. Maybe you're more of a TEDTalk junkie, or need some E E Cummings poetry to get your juices flowing. Either way, just as your environment can demotivate you and put your brain in conservation mode, it can also motivate you and light your brain right up.

Find your people

Time for more honesty. Writing this book has been one of the most mentally challenging things I've ever done, especially because I started writing a week before the COVID-19 pandemic lockdown. Schools closed, my three small children were at home 24/7, and my husband and I were both attempting to work full-time. By the time the kids were finally in bed, the last thing my brain wanted to do most days was sit in front of a screen and think of creative ways to make the inner workings of the human psyche interesting and easily digestible.

Knowing I need human connection to thrive, I got myself into a group of other badass women building, growing, and creating things while raising children during the global pandemic. Knowing there were other people who understood my situation who I could reach out to for support or a pep talk was everything. We humans need to know we are not alone.

If you're stepping up and stepping into your life in new and more challenging ways, find your people. People who understand you, who speak your language, who can remind you of your "why," and can speak life into you when you feel like trashing the whole thing.

TAKEAWAYS

- Motivation isn't automatic; it's manufactured (by you!).
- Managing your thoughts is necessary if you want to keep moving forward.
- Find your why and remind yourself of it often.
- Get support when you're doing something new and/or more challenging.

Journal prompt: What is my goal with engaging in this process? Why do I have it? Why is it important to me and what will make it worth the effort?

CHAPTER 9
ANGER

We all get angry, annoyed, or irritated sometimes—from a mild case of the grumps to full-on, steam-coming-out-of-our-ears fuming. We may be on a journey toward becoming more emotionally mature, but there will still be days when things irritate us to the core. Generally, anger is seen as a bad or negative emotion we should avoid at all costs (especially if you've been socialized as a woman). Over the years, I've often wondered why this is. It's clearly not a helpful or constructive expectation, especially since every human being on the planet feels angry sometimes—except maybe Mister Rogers. (I wonder if he ever totally lost his mind over anything? I can't picture it.)

Anger itself is often rooted in a sense of powerlessness, vulnerability, loss of control, or hurt. Some consider it a secondary emotion—which means it's there to mask another, more vulnerable emotion like fear or hurt. While this is often the case, anger can also just be anger.

As with all emotions, contrary to popular belief, anger is not good, bad, right, or wrong. Emotions give us information about what is consciously or subconsciously happening in our heads. Difficult emotions, including anger, are often a sign something important to us has been triggered, and we should pay attention to this.

And while there's nothing bad or wrong with *feeling* angry—common reactions (read: behaviors) to angry feelings can be unhelpful or destructive. Screaming at your kids, kicking the dog, or rear-ending someone for driving too slow are not really productive ways to express one's emotional state. And because anger is such an intense emotion, if we haven't learned how to deal with it constructively, the potential destruction of unchecked explosiveness can be catastrophic on many levels.

What is an emotional trigger?

An emotional trigger is a response to an activating event—including a memory—that sparks an intense emotional reaction, but is often disproportionate to the event itself. For example, someone doesn't text you back right away and you immediately get a deep, sinking feeling in your stomach because you're convinced that you're officially a reject. Or, as your colleague's presentation is getting oodles of praise from the group, you start to feel a wash of heat run from your head to your chest because your PowerPoint last week was barely commented on, and now you're convinced that you're failing at your job and no one likes you. You'll know you're being emotionally triggered when your fear response kicks in—i.e. your fight-or-flight response—and either your heart starts pounding, you start breathing in a shallow way, your stomach starts to flip, or your head gets hot and the tunnel vision sets in, but there isn't any actual danger present.

One such trigger happened recently for one of the women in my membership community, *The Shift Society*. She shared an instance when she found herself crying in the bathroom after a colleague raised their voice to her at work. While in hindsight, she knew her colleague wasn't being all that inappropriate, the slightly raised volume triggered an intense reaction she couldn't stop. After some reflection, she realized her response had nothing to do with work or her adult life at all. It had triggered a deep-seated childhood memory of a time when she lived in fear of her father, a raging alcoholic who came home many nights in a fit of screaming rage while she shook under her covers, anticipating the horror the night may bring.

When we're triggered in this way, we are rarely reacting to the circumstance in front of us; we are usually reacting to salt in a wound from our past. Our brain senses a threat and deduces that something terrible is coming as a subconscious memory of past pain or fear is summoned. We go into that fight-or-flight mode and, if left unprocessed, the intense emotional reaction will generate an equally charged behavior, like running to the bathroom in fear and crying uncontrollably.

When I imagine these triggers, I think of them as thorns piercing our skin with the butt end sticking slightly above the surface. When, intentionally or not, someone brushes up close to us and causes the thorn to press into us through our unresolved pain and unhealed shame, it doesn't take much for the pokey end to hit the sensitive spot and cause those emotions to flare.

And although it does not feel good to get poked, our triggers can be our teachers. When we have any kind of emotional reaction it's because something's been hit (or poked), and we can use that emotional reaction to get curious about what's behind it. It's important for us to understand our own triggers, so we can work through them, and eventually extract those thorns.

Take a few moments to think about the last time you were emotionally triggered—what did it feel like? Are you able to identify the past pain that incited it? Was your mind taken back to the origin of your emotional wound? Did it take time to figure out the root? Maybe you still don't know. And that's okay. Just take a moment to get curious and reflect.

All emotions are human emotions

The understanding that all emotions are human emotions is both helpful and healing, particularly because our instinct is to self-blame and self-shame when we experience emotional struggles. We can't stop ourselves from having emotional reactions, but we do have choices about how we act in response to our feelings. We don't need to throw a plate at the wall, scream at the dog, or snap at our partner. Instead, we can remember we are human, take a healing breath, and use the tools we know work. In this way, we take care of ourselves before we unleash on anyone (or anything) else. After all, it's likely that whoever we do unleash on will be someone we care deeply about.

It's funny how the people we love the most are the ones on the receiving end of our negative reactions and outbursts. Calling back to the concept of anger as a secondary emotion, when you direct your anger toward a loved one, it's not usually because they've done something horrible. More likely, you are experiencing emotional pain because you're not feeling heard, acknowledged, or understood in general. Then, within the relationship, there are little things happening that cause you to project *all* of your anger onto your friend. Perhaps there is division or disconnection in the relationship and in a backward (and exceedingly common) attempt to bring a person closer, anger and conflict is triggered and is combined with pent-up frustration about all the areas of your life where you don't feel seen or heard. This ends up exacerbating the issue with your friend and doesn't help you overcome the problems in your day-to-day life.

At times when you're triggered, it's imperative to remember that you have a choice. Instead of reacting with a nasty insult or a passive-aggressive remark, you can take a step back and use those curiosity skills you've been practicing. When you do that, you can communicate whatever you're thinking and feeling with calm, clarity, and respect—no beat-downs needed.

EXERCISE: BIG EMOTION TOOL—STOPP

So, how do you get yourself into a space of responding instead of reacting when you are experiencing a trigger? Enter, STOPP. This handy little tool will help you curb your fight-or-flight response. Whether your go-to is to battle it out or take the next train out, practicing STOPP will bring mindfulness to your responses in emotionally complex situations.

S—*Stop and take a breath.* When your intense emotions are triggered, don't forget to start with your breath. Take a big, deep, belly breath before you do anything else. This may be hard to remember if you're not used to it—it is in complete contradiction to your survival instinct when under duress—but it's worth it, I promise. It gives you something precious: time.

Intervening at a physiological level when your fight-or-flight response is activated is effective because fight or flight is a physiological response. When your brain is feeling threatened—whether real or imagined—telling yourself to let it go, not worry, or calm down isn't always enough. Logical thoughts have no place in primitive, automatic responses designed eons ago to keep you alive. Therefore, if you want access to the logical part of your brain, you have to respond to a physiological reaction with a physiological response, namely oxygen, which is exactly what breathing achieves!

T—*Tune into what you are feeling.* You're going to be so good at this one already. The second STOPP step takes you back to processing your emotions. After you stop (and breathe), you're going to ask yourself the following:

- What am I feeling right now?
- What does it feel like and where do I feel it in my body?
- What's the name of this emotion?

O—*Observe your thoughts.* After you process your emotions, you're going to ask yourself a few more questions:

- Why am I feeling this way?
- What just happened?
- What thoughts are going through my head about x experience?

These questions may be ringing a bell, and they should be, as this strategy fits in nicely with the ABCBO model. We find the consequential emotion first, and then think through the story we've created about it. The constant emphasis on reflection may seem like overkill, especially if it's difficult for you, but becoming more emotionally intelligent is inextricably tied to curiosity. If you never take the time to be curious about what you're thinking and feeling, the "why" behind your underlying emotions, or the pain from your past that might have followed you into the present, your emotional status may remain stunted. And if you wanted to be stunted, you wouldn't be reading this book.

PP—*Plan how you want to Proceed.* Now that you're calmer, grounded, and aware of your internal state, you can decide how to respond. How you want to handle it is up to you— and your logical thinking is available now that your conscious brain is accessible. This part is specifically tailored to you. The question I find most helpful in this stage is:

• What do I need?

Do you need to take a break so you don't say or do something you'll regret? Do you need time to sort through your thoughts? Do you need to get out of your head? Will going for a run or moving your body help you clear the brain fog? Do you need support or a vent session? When you take the time to plan, you will be more comfortable, confident, and clear when you do proceed.

When you **STOPP** regularly, not only will you have more tools to manage your emotions in the moment, but you're also training your brain to respond with mindfulness and intention in highly charged situations in the future. When you prove to your brain that you can drive yourself, even when venturing into bumpy territory, it starts to trust your navigation skills.

Move on from that anger

Most of us go through life lugging around bitterness and resentment. And though it may be warranted, none of it feels good. Some hang on to their grudges for a reason, but I'd venture that most people would rather feel free than travel around full of spite. If you're one of the latter, it's time to dive into the reasons behind our salty ways.

Expectations of others

We began to contemplate having high expectations of others when we talked about perfectionistic anxiety and discovered that unmet expectations are frequently the culprits of our resentment. When resentment is connected to an emotionally painful situation—especially if the pain continues to impact us in the present—it can be exceedingly difficult to move past it. On the lighter side, when your partner leaves their dirty clothes on the floor beside the basket instead of *in* the hamper, you can probably move past it in the moment, although small resentments may build unconsciously (because it's *not hard to just put them in!*). Either way, if a person, organization, or entity shouldn't have treated you *x* way, or done *y*, your lingering resentment is linked to nothing but your unmet expectations.

I've heard people say the secret to happiness is letting go of all expectations. But I have another idea about it. Managing expectations is not so much about not having any, but about understanding what the individual and relationship have to offer, and creating expectations based on that. I believe it's reasonable to expect my partner to comfort me when I'm sad and participate in parenting our children, but I cannot expect them to never make a mistake or stop their life every time I'm having a hard moment. To expect my staff to do the job they signed up for is reasonable, but I cannot expect that they will never need help, make no mistakes, or have zero questions. I expect my friends to put at least some effort into making time to spend together, but it would be defeatist for me to expect them to do this daily, considering our busy schedules. When it comes to expectations, having them isn't the problem—it's holding them higher than people are able or willing to live up to.

For any relationship to endure, some level of expectation must exist and be met. However, before we project expectations onto our relationships—you got it!—take some time to get curious about what your expectations are, what the person is offering, and how that fits together. What expectations can this person meet? What are they willing to do? What are they not able or willing to do within your relationship? Can they meet an expectation to a certain extent? And, if so, will that work for both of you?

It's important to get clear on what a person is willing and able to bring to a relationship instead of repeatedly upsetting yourself when they disappoint you. Maybe your parents will never be proud of you no matter how much you do or how successful you become, so if you stopped expecting them to express their pride, your relationship with them would be a lot less painful. Maybe your partner will never be able to keep to a tight budget, so instead of expecting them to pinch pennies, figure out a different way to divide your finances.

Of course, certain unmet expectations can be deal-breakers. Relationships sometimes run their course and there is no shame in releasing a relationship if necessary. Friends can become neglectful, significant others can break trust, family members can be abusive, and work colleagues can be bullies. Differentiating between reasonable deal-breakers and unreasonable expectations is part of the work you're doing.

Life not going according to plan

Consciously or unconsciously, we all have plans about how things should and will go in our lives. When we should get the promotion, the age and way we should find love, the number of friends we should have, and how crazy-fun our annual summer barbeque should be—we walk through life with plans, and when they don't go accordingly, we feel disappointed, angry, and bitter. The problem with unmet expectations goes beyond our relationships.

Just like with other people, it's fine to have ideas, hopes, and preferences, but when you dwell on the way things should have happened but didn't, we're only making our own lives harder. However, if you let yourself be present to what is, instead of focusing on what isn't, life automatically gets a little (or a lot) better. Perhaps there's something you can do to increase the chances of the outcome you want, or perhaps you'll find peace in what's available now. When you are the driver of your human experience, you know things don't always have to go your way in order for you to be okay. So, if you planned a big dinner party at your house and several people didn't show, and the few who did come didn't bring what you asked them to, it's okay. Life will go on and you will have *fun*, but only if you let yourself enjoy the party the way it came together instead of dwelling on the fact that you had six salads and only one small dessert. And hey, it just means everyone left a little healthier than when they came!

Empathy

Time to switch gears from understanding anger to figuring out how to make friends with it. Being less reactive to your anger is great, but being kind to yourself when it comes up is some next-level skills. Remember self-compassion? Next time you're angry, interrupt the cycle of reprimanding yourself for feeling it—which, as you know, only makes everything worse—and speak to yourself with understanding using your anti-shame script. *It's understandable I was feeling angry because I've been under a lot of pressure at work and was worn thin by the end of the day.*

This doesn't mean raging out when you were overwhelmed was a great choice, but beating yourself up when you make a mistake only increases the likelihood the cycle will repeat itself. When you blame and berate yourself, you create your own shame and compromise your mental capacity to dig deep and understand the real issue (i.e., taking on too much at work) and plan to address the problem (i.e. set healthier boundaries with your boss), which would decrease your overwhelm and leave you with more energy to deal with your other stressors.

Beyond self-compassion lies empathy. Remember that fellow commuter with the rude gestures and honking? They, too, may be acting out their anger due to something in their internal state and may not have the skills to sort themselves out. People generally don't suck on purpose. Everyone has their own pain, issues, vulnerabilities, and unresolved hurt. Empathy isn't excusing harmful behavior, but coming from a place of understanding helps us.

I had someone in my life once who often incited both hurt and anger in me with their words, attitude, and even their scoffs. Although it was tempting to constantly vent about them or sulk about their most recent insult, I decided to work hard to think differently about them. I reminded myself they had demons and pain they didn't know how to manage, so myself and those of us around them were experiencing the outcome of that. Sure, I didn't like the way they dealt with their internal struggles, so I set clear boundaries for myself in the relationship around how vulnerable I'd be with them or close I'd get to them, but having empathy for their struggles allowed me to not take their outbursts personally and was powerful not for them—although perhaps they sensed a shift—but for me.

TAKEAWAYS

- Think of anger as a helpful signal about what's going on inside of you instead of as a shameful or unnatural emotion.
- Getting curious about your anger is a crucial way to turn it around.
- Use STOPP as a tool to understand your anger and turn it into a constructive response.
- Be kind to yourself and others, for we are all human beings with human feelings, even when mistakes are made.

Journal prompt: What do I expect of others in my relationships that may be unreasonable? What would happen if I stopped expecting something they aren't willing or able to give me?

CHAPTER 10
GUILT

Guilt (aka Big G) is a major topic in mental health, and something many people struggle to navigate, whether on the giving or the receiving end of the deal. What is guilt? Simply put, guilt is the emotion that shows up when we think we've done something bad, wrong, or harmful. Honestly, it can be a great barometer in interpersonal relationships. If you never felt bad after doing something bad, it would mean you had no capacity for empathy. Do you know who has no capacity for empathy? Sociopaths.

When used properly, guilt will help us pause, take a step back, question our behavior, and inspect our actions. It can help curb future harming behavior in a preventative way. You wouldn't want to cheat a client, lie to your partner, or call in sick to go for a hike on the day your whole team was relying on you because you'd feel terrible if you did, and even worse if you got caught.

Several years ago, I was on my way to meet a friend for happy hour after work when I saw my boss walking straight toward me. This wouldn't have been a problem, but the moment our eyes met, the color drained from her face, as I'm sure surprise and confusion spread over mine. That morning, she'd called me with a husky voice to request I pass along the message that she couldn't get out of bed. Whoops!

Guilt can also incentivize us to change our behavior after doing something unhelpful or harmful. One day I was turning left into a crosswalk and, as I turned, I came close to hitting a pedestrian and had to slam on my brakes. The terror in their eyes at this close call spurred deep guilt in me, and I've triple-checked for crossing pedestrians every single time I've made a left turn since.

On the flip side of its potential helpfulness, however, guilt can be destructive when used as a form of self-punishment. When you feel too much guilt after a mistake and use it as a determinate of your own lack of worth, it's nothing but your old frenemy Shame wearing a shoddy mask.

EXERCISE: WORDS OF COMPASSION AND UNDERSTANDING

Use this exercise when you're carrying around guilt for past transgressions you just can't seem to shake. This isn't making excuses for past hurtful behaviors; it's showing compassion to an earlier version of yourself who made a choice functioning from the level of awareness they had at that time. It's understanding that your best changes day to day, moment to moment.

Start with breath. In. Out. In. Out.

And say or read to yourself: *I see you and, more than anyone else, I see what you were going through when you* [insert source of overly guilty thoughts and feelings]. *Even if it wasn't the wisest, best, or most honorable choice, it was what you did at the time. You're a human being who makes mistakes, but making mistakes doesn't mean you're a bad person. Instead of continuing to focus on the past, I'm going to make a new commitment now. I commit to working on better as I move forward. I commit to being mindful with my choices and actions, and learning from any missteps I make. I commit to taking responsibility for the mistakes I make and being more forgiving toward myself when I do.*

You can work through this exercise in your head or on paper as many times as you need. Give yourself permission to finally move forward.

Using guilt

Aside from self-inflicted punishment, guilt is also misused when attempted as a strategy for emotional manipulation. For example, imagine if you call your mom and the first thing she says is, "Oh, it's you. I haven't heard from you in forever. I thought maybe you'd lost my number!" You're immediately annoyed and frustrated, and you think, *There Mom goes—making me feel all guilty again! I can't ever do enough for her!*

But see the fallacy here? We all know now that Mom is not the one making you feel guilty. If you break down the ABCBO chart on this, what do you think you'll find is making you feel guilty? You got it. Your thoughts. You're feeling annoyed because you think you've done something wrong based on her comments. Truth-bomb time: Your mom's distress because you don't call her as much as she wants doesn't mean you've done anything fundamentally wrong. You just haven't done what she wanted you to do. She *attempted* to make you feel guilty—which wasn't the most emotionally mature move on her part—but now that you know how to manage your mind using the ABCBO model, you're not going to get sucked into it.

Many of us are used to thinking if someone doesn't like something we've done, it means we've done something wrong, which triggers guilty feelings. I want to invite you to a new kind of life, one where you take a step back and own the fact that as a grown human being with mastery over their life and time, you get to decide how often you call your mom (or anyone else).

You are allowed to call people when you want to call them even if it's not when they want you to call. You are allowed to use your time as you choose. And others are allowed to not like it. They might have expectations they may want to adjust so they stop making themselves feel so terrible—as do you.

Once you make peace with your decisions, comments like this one won't bring up guilt anymore. You can be empathic and understanding of failing someone else's expectation without it meaning you've done anything wrong. It can be tempting to believe it's your responsibility to make everyone around you happy or prevent them from ever feeling upset, but it's not. Do you know what's making other people unhappy or upset? Their thoughts.

Don't turn it around

To flip the script, guilt isn't helpful when *we* use it manipulatively on others either. Communicating in roundabout or passive-aggressive ways are a shortcut to inauthenticity, which is the opposite of the work you're doing here. Guilt-tripping as a backdoor method to get what we want isn't more acceptable when you do it to others than when someone does it to you.

A few months ago, I came home after a long day of work to the kitchen looking like the aftermath of a police raid. Everything was in complete disarray. I was exhausted. When I saw the kitchen countertops littered with the remains of dinner and crumbs all over the floor, I was immediately irritated, annoyed, and frustrated with my husband. (So many thoughts and feelings. So many.) I had to come home to a disaster in the kitchen, the kids' lunches still needed to be prepped, I had paperwork to finish, and to me, it seemed as if I was the only one who cared.

But instead of using all the tools and strategies I promote to my clients and students—and because I didn't want to overtly nag, I defaulted to guilt-trippy and manipulative. Huffing and puffing as I began to collect the remains of what I assumed was something that used to be edible, I mumbled under my breath, "Sure. I'd love to clean up all of this mess even though I'm so tired I can't see straight," as I banged around some pots and pans. (Read: I was definitely being loud enough for my husband in the next room to hear.)

My husband could have easily reacted, taken the bait, and we would have ended the evening with a full-fledged conflict. Instead, he walked over from the other room and asked, "Would you like my help?" Snapped out of my passive-aggressive daze, I gladly accepted, to which he replied, "I'm happy to. But maybe next time when you want something you just ask me?"

Ooofff. Checkmate. Sometimes, asking for what we need seems so much more difficult in our minds than in reality. We all need reminders, especially when our personal history is triggered, or we are emotionally depleted. I grew up in a family with high, often upspoken, expectations—but we all knew what they were. Guilt trips were rampant and are part of my primitive wiring. However, I married someone whose background is quite different than mine, and who does not play into guilt. Thankfully for me, this particular difference and the obnoxiously long hours I've spent studying the topic have taught me how to communicate like a grown-up (most of the time).

Guilt doesn't feel good on either end of the spectrum— giving or receiving—but we learned to use it for a reason. You may have grown up in a home where it wasn't safe for you to be open and honest in your communication, so sharing your thoughts and feelings directly is exceedingly uncomfortable for you. Back-door, sneaky communication methods may have been the only way you were able to get your wants and needs met as a child. Perhaps the adults in your life modeled guilt as a manipulation strategy, so it makes sense that your brain logged this information away. Maybe you have no idea why guilt is one of your modes of communication, but you know it's unhealthy and you want to be able to express yourself more honestly.

Regardless of how, why, or where you learned to manipulate or communicate using guilt, you can unlearn it with practice. When you practice being more honest and direct, clean, clear, and classy communication will become your *modus operandi*, even when your kitchen is an utter shambles upon your arrival home.

How to say "no" without feeling guilty

All right, let's be real. Saying no is hard. Not in the literal sense necessarily, but in the oh-my-gosh-what-if-they-hate-me? sense. There's a reason—often several—we don't say no. And these reasons are usually tied to the avoidance of feeling guilty. As a result, we say yes to things we don't want to do and feel all kinds of anger and stress, among other emotions, because we feel put-upon and *made* to do something we didn't want to do in the first place.

Ready to read something you might not like?

You don't say "no" because you're more comfortable feeling resentment toward someone else than experiencing guilt within yourself. It's easier to blame someone for "making you do something you didn't want to do" than feel guilty for disappointing the same person by declining the request. Raise your hand if you've ever played the blame game instead of taking ownership of your own time and energy needs and preferences! You can't see it, but I'm raising both my hands again.

Here's the problem: When you don't take just as much responsibility of your No as you do your Yes, you're getting in your own way. Remember how you get to decide how you want to spend your own time and energy? When you say yes to something you don't want to do, it's as if you're saying no to something you do want to do. In other words, you're lying to everyone, including yourself. Stop. It's hurting you and it's hurting your relationships.

Although Cousin Sarah might be upset if you don't give up your entire weekend to help her move, if you say yes begrudgingly, your thoughts and feelings surrounding the event are likely to have a bitter tinge. Instead of laughing while you're awkwardly hauling the couch down the stairs, you'll be predisposed for many more negative emotions, which may not only impact your weekend, but also dampen her excitement about her new place. As an extension of processing your thoughts and feelings, pay attention to your real yesses and your fake noes. Of course there are times when we "take one for the team" and do things for a loved one we'd rather not, but as long as you change your thoughts about it and decide that even though fulfilling their request would not be your first choice on how you wanted to spend your day, you're okay with doing it because sometimes that's just what we do for the people we love. But take heed, my friend: Make sure you figure out which thoughts to think so you are able to honestly be okay with fulfilling the ask so you don't drag any resentment into the favor fulfillment with you.

Being clear with your wants (or *do not* wants), if you're not used to it, can be like learning to parallel park a bus on a city street—absolutely agonizing. With that in mind, be kind to yourself. It can be overwhelming when you flex new skills that feel foreign to your personal experience, so start small with safe people and go at your own pace.

TAKEAWAYS

- Guilt can be a helpful emotion when it's used as a transformative tool coupled with curiosity to make positive changes.
- Don't use guilt to meet your needs in relationships— you're worthy of giving and receiving open and honest communication and so are your loved ones.
- Practice saying "no" without feeling guilty. (It can be hard!)

Journal prompt: When do I feel overly guilty? Is it necessary? What would happen if I stopped feeling guilty when I haven't done anything bad or wrong?

CHAPTER 11
LONELINESS

Loneliness is on the rise in the Western world and the repercussions are serious. We may no longer require other people for baseline survival, but we seem to forget we are creatures with a need for deep interpersonal connection. And as we become more digitally connected, our relational connections become less substantial. (It's tough to build those same in-person bonds through words on a screen.) The consequences of loneliness are significant for both mental and physical health. While it's pretty obvious being alone for too long can eventually make even the most independent person feel anxious or depressed, loneliness is also associated with illnesses such as diabetes, high blood pressure, obesity, and heart disease.

Alfred Adler, one of the forefathers of modern psychology and a colleague of Sigmund Freud, had his own theory of the roots of human suffering. He believed all humans have a deep desire to belong, going so far as to say that genuine human connection is as essential to human survival as air and water. He also hypothesized that most of human suffering is rooted in our fear of being imperfect. According to Adler, many of our struggles come from the fear of rejection if people see who we really are—and we'll find out we are as unlovable and unworthy as we fear deep down that we are.

Ultimately, loneliness (and the accompanying issues) is about disconnection. This is exactly why everything Adler wrote is so important to remember. When you feel emotionally disconnected from those around you, the consequences of this are real.

This disconnection can come in the form of becoming these other versions of yourself through people-pleasing, performing, and perfecting to prove your worthiness of love and belonging. It can also come in the form of a never-ending cycle: The lonelier we feel, the more thoughts we have about being unlovable, which results in us feeling unlovable, which decreases the likelihood we will reach out to connect with others. When this happens, we stay stuck, disconnected, and lonely.

However, your saving grace is your truly authentic relationships. You know the relationships I mean, right? I'm talking about your people. The ones who see you, understand you, and love you for being you—nothing more, nothing less. You know, your "hide-a-body" friends you could call in the middle of the night and they'd show up right away with a shovel, no questions asked.

If you have at least one relationship like this, I hope you consider yourself one of the luckiest humans on the planet. Few things are more important than existing alongside someone with whom you truly belong. And by "belong," I don't mean "fit in." There's an important difference between the two.

A big part of being human is wanting—no, *needing*—to feel valued, worthy, and lovable. This basic need can be traced back to the more ancient need for survival. And now, it's about more than just safety; it's being accepted and loved as your true self. However, we often confuse the concept of belonging with the unconscious tendency to fit in. As Brené Brown so beautifully articulates in *The Gifts of Imperfection*, "Fitting in is about assessing a situation and becoming who you need to be to be accepted. Belonging, on the other hand, doesn't require us to change who we are; it requires us to *be* who we are."

Many of us have been trying to do everything we can, maybe even for our whole lives, just to fit in. We pretend to like things we don't, become people we're not, be okay when we aren't, tacitly agree when we want to protest, and say "Yes" when we mean "No." When we confuse fitting in with belonging, there is a desperation that comes over us because we don't think who we are is good enough. We think if we can just manage to be who other people want us to be, we will be liked, approved of, and accepted.

Fitting in gets messy in a way true belonging doesn't. When I act and perform as the person others want me to be in order to gain approval, love, and acceptance, I may get what I wanted, but I still won't feel belonging. When we please, perfect, and perform to earn someone's love, the person who is accepted and loved is not the real us. It doesn't feel good because the authentic version of us is still hiding behind the approval-seeking part of us, so we continue to feel a lack of belonging. When we are inauthentic, so are the connections we make, which brings us back to the starting line where we feel lonely, disconnected, undervalued, and invisible.

True belonging begins with courage. The courage to be ourselves and believing we are worthy just as we are. When we find and foster genuine relationships, we form a sense of true belonging. And when we belong, while loneliness may still visit, it won't be a permanent passenger.

EXERCISE: LEARN TO LOVE AND ACCEPT YOURSELF

Ask yourself: *What choices would I make, what would I do or try, and how would I show up differently if I truly believed in my inherent worth?*

Loaded question, huh? As we move toward self-acceptance and look at what we do or don't do because we believe we are unworthy and not good enough, answering it will be easier. Many times, shame shows up when we're setting goals, dreaming about the future, and pushing our potential.

Experiences we desire, people we want to connect with, feelings we want to share, and self-imposed limits we want to nudge past seem to be far beyond the horizon. But if we keep driving toward self-acceptance, we will slowly approach a life in which we understand the worth and value we bring just through being our authentic selves.

So, if you knew you were inherently worthy, what choices would you make? What would you do? How would you show up? If you knew that no matter what happened and what anyone else thought, you would still love and accept yourself, what would you try?

Answer the questions. And when you do, listen. You can make change. And you can start today.

Digital distance

When I consider how digitally connected everyone is in the present, I can't help but think this is one of the reasons we're facing loneliness to such a large extent. Although it seems like everyone knows what's going on with everyone else, the digital distance makes it so we are far less emotionally connected with other humans. It's almost as if because our family and friends are constantly in our pockets, we don't feel the need to reach out to them in person the way humans did for years.

Screens and technology come between humans and we don't even realize it (or perhaps we do). When you can frame yourself in any way you want, add filters, and edit everything you put out in the world, there's a falseness to the "reality" you present. With social media, you can re-type and re-record anything and everything depending on if you want to present as the interesting, thoughtful, deep, or witty person you wish you were in real time.

With curated words and tuned-up selfies come the loss of making genuine, imperfect connections. The kind you make by commiserating over a bad hair day or accidentally saying something awkward. Or when everyone realizes these things are completely normal and you don't feel quite as alone. Technology is impacting what used to be typical opportunities for vulnerability and authenticity, so the increase in loneliness is no surprise.

Does it have to be this way?

Getting out

Loneliness is an isolating, vulnerable experience that feels terrible. If you guessed I was going to say working through it begins with your thoughts, you're starting to get the hang of this! Yes, working intentionally to have thoughts will allow you to create the feelings that will drive your behaviors to give you the outcome you're hoping for (i.e., being less lonely!).

For example, instead of thinking, *I'm not very interesting*, which may induce sadness, so you stay home on Saturday night listening to emo music in your joggers, practice choosing to think something like, *I can be really funny and I tell great stories. I usually have a good time once I get myself out of the house.* This train of thought is much more likely to have you hopping in the shower to clean up for a night out on the town during which you're more likely to have fun with others over the course of the evening. Mission accomplished.

Get vulnerable

Daring to be your true self to enable authentic connection with other people can feel scary. We make ourselves vulnerable when we open the door of our lives and ask someone to come along for the ride, hoping they'll love us through thick and thin for exactly who we are. Some people you meet along your journey may be able to do that, and others will not. There will be people who love you for who you are for them, not for who you are as a person. People who, if you decide you no longer want to perform how they wish, may reject you completely.

I know this sounds intimidating, but don't let it deter you. There can be a cost that comes with authentic, honest connection, but the detriment of inauthenticity and disconnection is even greater. Don't perpetuate loneliness and disconnection because you're unwilling to allow anyone to see your imperfections. Connection takes courage and I know you have it in you.

How do we deal with loneliness?

One of my all-time favorite quotes was said by Maya Angelou in her 1973 interview with Bill Moyers: "You only are free when you realize you belong no place—you belong every place—no place at all. The price is high. The reward is great." When we learn how to value and belong to ourselves, we take our belonging everywhere we go, because we take ourselves wherever we go.

I've noticed that when I'm taking good care of myself, listening to myself, trusting myself, and feeling connected to who I truly am, I can walk into any room and talk to anyone. I can be anywhere and be comfortable and confident. I don't need anyone else's approval, because I approve of me, and that's what matters most.

When I'm connected within, not only do I stop seeking approval, but I also find it so much easier to make true connections with others. It makes sense. I don't know about you, but I'm naturally drawn to people who are centered, confident, and seem to know themselves. It's as if being connected and comfortable with oneself is contagious. When I'm near it, it's easier to stand tall, exhale fully, and be happy with who I am, too.

When you build a relationship with yourself, you show up differently in any social situation and in your relationships. Because when you belong to yourself, you belong everywhere you go. When you enter a room knowing you belong—because you always belong to yourself—you will be more easily and genuinely welcomed. And when the true, authentic you is in the driver's seat, why would you ever feel alone?

TAKEAWAYS

- Let's all embrace our need to be seen for who we truly are.
- Be aware of your brain bias to "fit in," which is different than to "belong."
- Learn to love and accept yourself for who you are now.
- Strengthening your relationship with yourself will strengthen your relationships with others; it is the antidote to loneliness.

Journal prompt: What stops me from showing up as my authentic self? What thoughts and beliefs would allow me to show up authentically more often?

PART THREE

BECOME THE DRIVER OF YOUR OWN THOUGHTS

Why did you say that? That was so stupid.
They probably think you're a loser now.
"You should have just kept your mouth shut. What's wrong with you?
People will stop hanging out with you if you can't figure out how to just go with the flow.

Any of this self-talk sound familiar? Similar to something we've been over before when we tripped over our own feet in front of someone, huh? Have you ever spent hours after a social gathering ruminating about what other people might be thinking about you? Kicking yourself for the way you expressed your opinion, a joke you told, or a comment you made because you're not 100 per cent sure *they took it the way you meant it?*

If you've answered yes, I have a few things to tell you: a) it doesn't really matter in the grand scheme of things, b) it's kind of egocentric to think a person is obsessing over something you said, c) if someone is judging you, more often than not, it's just a deflection of their own insecurities, and d) most people are not spending their post-party hours thinking about you at all. You know why? They're probably in their own home after the party trying to deduce how you're judging them for whatever they said. Facts. We spend so much time worrying about what people think about us, but the truth is, most of the time they're not. And if they are, it's not long before their own egocentric brain is back to thinking about themselves and/or what you might be thinking about them!

So why do we care so much about what others think about us? Like many things brain-related, it starts at your beginning. There's that foundation again. Man, do the reverberations of it reach far and wide. If you find yourself worrying (excessively) about what other people think, one or more of the following may describe your childhood and/or family experience when you were growing up:

- Love was transactional depending upon your behavior, attitude, adherence to rules, etc.
- Ideas, opinions, or life choices outside the "norm" by you or others in your immediate family were punished or highly criticized.
- Your parents openly judged and harshly criticized others—usually covertly behind their backs—with ideas, opinions, or life choices that diverged from theirs (that were, again, primarily just deflections of their own insecurities).
- Your choices were heavily controlled, and you were rarely allowed to make your own decisions, perhaps even through adolescence and into adulthood.
- Your parents were worried about what other people thought about them.

Basically, if you were raised to value other people's opinions of you more than your own, whether through expectation or modeling, it's no wonder you still do.

Becoming a deeply confident adult and driving your own bus is about letting other people have their own opinions about any given topic, including any given part of you, and maintaining your ability to self-differentiate. The Bowen Theory is based on the principle that we all must allow ourselves to have our own thoughts, opinions, ideas, and perspectives—and extend this same courtesy to others.

Emotional fusion, the inverse of self-differentiation in this theory, is where many of us are based on our personal background. When you are engaging in emotional fusion, your emotional state is so connected to someone else's that your level of emotional function is dependent not only on theirs, but on their perception of yours. If they're not okay, you're not okay—and if they think you're not okay, you're also not okay. See how this can get messy?

I'm not saying you should turn into a raging narcissist who doesn't care about anyone else. But I am suggesting you spend a little more time getting clear on what you think about you and a little less time worrying about what thoughts about you could possibly be floating around in others' brains.

Another key to driving your own bus is picking apart all the self-defeating thoughts that make your life harder. Do you have a greatest hits list of these thoughts like me? Some my brain likes to throw at me when I'm already feeling down are, *No one really likes me, I don't have what it takes*, and, *I'm not good/smart/funny/interesting/capable/cool enough.*

It's safe to say any thought starting with "I'm not" and ending with "enough" is likely not a helpful thought. And you know what? They can all go straight in the bin. Instead of sparking joy, thoughts like these drive you to question your worthiness, hold you back, and keep you stuck. You have no place for them in your brain anymore. So, right now, toss "I'm not good enough," "I'm not smart enough," "I'm not pretty enough," and "I'm not brave enough" into the trash along with those back issues of teen bop magazines you're saving for some unknown reason.

Now that we've cleaned things up, we're going to dive into where these self-defeating beliefs come from in the first place, since you weren't born with them. (As the parent of three small children, I can tell you infants are never worried about being judged, even when they fill their pants daily and scream for seven of their twelve waking hours.) And then we're going to figure out exactly what to do with them so you can stop the endless loop of self-doubt. Let's get to it.

CHAPTER 12

"I HAVE A CRITICAL VOICE IN MY HEAD"

We all have one. If you're lucky, you have one inner critic in your brain whose only purpose is to criticize and bring you down. The rest of us are driving around an entire committee. You know that voice (or voices) that buckles itself in firmly between your ears and leads the *Not Enough* parade? Not smart enough, not strong enough, not brave enough, not capable enough, not fit enough, not interesting enough, not attractive enough, not lovable enough. Never enough.

Whose thoughts are they?

If you weren't born with a carful of critics, where do they come from, when did they start talking to you, and why? Whether you were directly or indirectly taught, your thoughts about not being good enough came from someone or somewhere else. Not you.

Because our greatest influencers as children are our parents, it's likely many of these ideas came from them, even if it wasn't intentional. It's funny. It wasn't until I became a parent that I fully realized parents are just people who are older than their children. That's it. They don't know everything, they don't have all the answers, and they aren't experts on being human.

When I had this realization, I also understood my own parents weren't right about everything—including their thoughts and perspective about who I am. They have their own ideas about who I am, but only some of them are accurate.

Perhaps as a child you saw people you looked up to being unnecessarily hard on themselves and figured that was how you were supposed to treat yourself, too. Perhaps you were mistreated as a child, and your inner critic was your brain's way of trying to rationalize it. When harmful things happen to children and they don't understand why, their brains try to make sense of it, as brains will do. Young brains, which are egocentric by nature, often conclude the mistreatment is their fault and they deserve it. There's no other explanation available to them—because grown-ups are supposed to know best. And, voila, a shame is born.

To be fair to parents and caretakers, though, you likely internalized these self-defeating messages from other places as well. You have been absorbing ideas and ideals from your environment and culture since the day you were born. Some of them have been helpful to you, like, "Treat others how you'd like to be treated." Others, like, "You'll finally be beautiful if you buy this snail mucin face mask," not so much. You were exposed to a steady stream of explicit and implicit messages about your gender, color, sexual orientation, size, shape, body ability, status, level of intelligence, degree of attractiveness, and much more. You were also told which things about you were and were not good enough. And if you're human, at least one part of you is different than what is considered "ideal." With this messaging coming from all directions, everyone is bound to question their worth at some point.

Here's an interesting thing. Your inner critic is shaped from what you were taught, what you absorbed, and what you internalized. Essentially, you inherited and learned thoughts and beliefs about who you are, what you deserve, and who you're *allowed* to be. This means, though, none of these are your thoughts. None of them.

These thoughts and beliefs were formed inside your brain—usually in childhood during your "form"-ative years (Get it?). Your brain was taking in all kinds of information about how to think about yourself, others, life, and the world. Just because those thoughts were formed at some point because someone said something to, about, or around us, they're not written in stone, and they don't have to stay. That's right. They can be removed and replaced. And if this is true (which it is... because science) it means you can *choose* how you want to think about yourself.

Time to redecorate

Think of your brain as a house. When you were young, without you even realizing what was happening, several people who you believed to be experts decorated your house. Each design element they incorporated, from the wall art to the dining chairs, was truly what they thought should go in your house. And now you're an adult, but you've left everything exactly the same for years.

What if you stopped to ask yourself if you even like the set-up? Are you really into the fixtures and furniture someone else chose? Would you have picked the current color palette? If not, what do you want to see in there? What's your taste? You're allowed to decorate your brain house whichever way *you* want it to be. You can choose how and what you want to think about yourself, others, life, and the world around you. You are the interior designer of your own mind, no matter what you were told about the importance and permanence of the initial décor.

Detaching from thoughts

Okay. You know where your thoughts about yourself came from, you're starting to think about whether the thoughts you were given are keepers, and so it's time to break your brain a little.

We've established that it's probable many of the things you think about yourself didn't originate with you. Taking it one step further, you are not your thoughts anyways. Regardless of what's rumbling around in your head, *you are not your thoughts*. You are the one *thinking* your thoughts.

What are you talking about, Julia? I know. Stay with me.

I'll say it again: *You are not your thoughts. You are the conscious being thinking your thoughts.* Boom. And how do we know this? Because you can think about thinking. You can literally pause and contemplate the thoughts going through your mind at any moment. Try it right now. What are you thinking about? And what do you think about what you're thinking about? It's a brain-twister, but it's what's happening.

Our emotional experience as human beings is created by our thoughts. So much so that becoming more in charge of our thoughts is key to becoming more in charge of our emotions. Part of being behind the wheel of your thoughts is resisting the temptation to believe every single notion that enters your brain.

Detaching from your thoughts is about taking a step back, observing what your brain is doing, and deciding how much you want to go along with whatever is going on. When you can detach, you can decide what thoughts you will keep without making a whole big fuss. Cultivating unattached observation moves you away from automatic belief in what you think and creates space between you and your thoughts. It quietens your mind, and helps you to be present enough to avoid getting caught up in your head.

Creating this space in the mind is a simple concept, but it can get complicated. Our brains—especially in their primitive state—are much more comfortable reacting than responding. However, when we go with our knee-jerk reaction in non-life-or-death situations, this can (and likely will) backfire. When we build our detachment skills, we are building our ability to *respond* instead. And when we respond, we are not only giving ourselves time to make decisions about our behavior, but also time to decide what we think about our thoughts and act accordingly.

A little while ago, I wanted to surprise a dear friend of mine with an extravagant birthday gift, but to pull off the surprise, I needed to enlist her husband in a stealthy collaboration. I sat down to write him an email laying out all the glorious details, hit send, and then eagerly awaited his reply. I was so excited and could hardly wait to be met with (almost) same-level excitement from him. When he replied the next day, I was immediately deflated upon reading the first line. "It's a nice idea, but…"— followed by many more buts. The exhilaration that had me floating on cloud nine over the previous few days morphed into a sinking feeling of disappointment.

Here's the interesting thing. My reaction to his email wasn't disappointment merely because he wasn't on board with executing this epic plan. In fact, it was hardly that at all. My brain immediately turned on me with a plethora of self-criticism. *Ugh. I'm sure he thinks this is so stupid. I'm a loser. He probably thinks she wouldn't even want to take a big birthday trip with me anymore and is just trying to kybosh the plan to save her from something so stupid.* No joke—this is what I thought (and much more like it).

I wish I could tell you I immediately caught the absurdity of my thinking, especially seeing as this woman has been my bestie since we were 17 years old. But, alas, I cannot, as the human brain isn't always so reasonable. After this blow to my self-esteem brought on by nothing but my own thoughts and several mentally tortuous minutes, I was able to take a breath and a step back. Only then was I able to see what was happening and change my thoughts, which went something like, *Okay. These thoughts are about what I'm making his email mean about me, which is making me feel terrible! My thoughts are the only thing creating all of this drama. I don't have to believe them just because they exist.*

Now that I was calm, I was able to consider alternate reasons his response was not the one I'd wanted and expected him to give. He could have been worried about surprising her because he wasn't sure if she'd want time to plan and prepare for a trip away. He could have been apprehensive about planning a big trip in the middle of the fall when they have three kids who have weekend activities on the schedule. He could have been worried their kids would be upset about her going away without them on a big fun trip. *He* could have wanted to go away somewhere with her for her birthday. They could have already talked about what she wanted to do to celebrate.

See how many other options my brain had to choose from? And I only named a few. Whatever I was thinking about his email were optional thoughts, not necessarily truths. To take it one step further, even if his reasoning was somewhat aligned with my original thought process—he didn't think his wife would want to go on a birthday trip with me for one reason or another—it still doesn't mean I'm a stupid loser. Again, those are optional thoughts in my brain about what the refusal means about me. They aren't facts. Disinterest or decline is not a reflection of my worthiness as a human being, just as whatever your brain defaults to after similar disappointments is not a reflection of yours.

CHAPTER 13
"THIS IS PERSONAL"

Taking things personally. Ouf. This is such a tough one. The human brain has a funny little way of making things so much more about us than they really are, doesn't it? Truth bomb: nothing is personal. Even if someone does something hurtful and follows up their transgression by actually stating, "This is personal," it's still not. Every action a person takes is based on their own thoughts and feelings. Their *own* thoughts. They are making behavior choices because of what they are thinking— even if what they are thinking about is you, their thoughts are still their own.

In general, everyday life, most people aren't exacting elaborate plans against you. They are doing things for themselves based on what they want, need, and think. Has your boss ever been snappy with you, after which you thought it was probably because they don't like you or you did something wrong? What would you think if you knew they'd had a fight with their partner at home that same morning? Don Miguel Ruiz, in his international classic *The Four Agreements*, outlines this concept wonderfully: "Nothing others do is because of you. What others say and do is a projection of their own reality." In other words, their actions stem from their thoughts (just like your actions stem from yours).

Thought investigator

Another example from my own experience—taking things personally was a regular occurrence for me before I learned how to manage my mind—happened when a friend of mine was visiting from out of town. Knowing when they were arriving, I texted them excitedly only to find out they'd made other plans during the only times I was free (and which I'd communicated to them weeks prior). And although my brain could have interpreted this turn of events in many different ways, such as them assuming my schedule was flexible, so we'd be able to figure out a different time to get together, or they'd forgotten when I'd be free, or we'd had a miscommunication somewhere along the way, none of these more reasonable options was where I went. Nope, not my brain. My brain was all, *Oh my gosh. They don't even value my time. They probably don't even care to see me. They never cared about me anyways.*

Now, there is plenty of evidence that points to the fact that this person loves and values me, although in that moment my brain was trying to convince me otherwise. Thankfully, I was able to catch my sneaky self-shaming brain before it got out of control and ask myself the ultimate why. Why was my brain interpreting this small situation as a serious threat to my lovability? Now that I'd taken a moment, the answer came quickly.

I realized, though unrelated, this was triggering an emotional memory of one of the most painful things I've been through. When I was in high school, I had the agonizing experience of living a modified plot of *Mean Girls*. One day, seemingly out of nowhere, all of my besties decided I was a loser and would no longer be a member of our girl group. I was out. Just like that. Not a single friend left. Not only was I out, but I was also the target of months of ridicule, rumors, and bullying from this group of girls I'd considered my ride-or-dies. Then, as an adult, when my friend didn't have time for me like I'd hoped, my brain connected this to my experience of being ostracized. Funnily enough, she'd mixed up the times I was free on her calendar, so, contrary to my original thoughts, my lovability hadn't actually been on the brink of extinction. Thank goodness I didn't let my brain run away with that train, huh?

Our big emotional reactions aren't usually about the event itself; they're about what we think the situation means about *us*. My reaction wasn't merely based on my thinking that my friend didn't care about me; it was that I thought if it was true it would mean I was unlovable. When you're tempted to take something personally, never underestimate the power of asking yourself, *What are my other thought options?*

EXERCISE: HOW TO "DEPERSONALIZE" SOMETHING

When you are in the habit of taking things personally, there's a simple method you can turn to for "depersonalization":

1. Think about a situation that personally offended you—a time you thought someone did or said something to slight you.
2. Now take a minute or two to consider what other explanations you can give for their actions that are not about you.
   - Is it possible the person who upset you was having a bad day and was taking out their emotions on you?
   - Is it possible the person was unaware they were speaking or acting in a way you may have interpreted as offensive?
   - Could you have interpreted what they said, did, declined, etc. to be about you when it wasn't?

---

3. Explore and write down five options that could explain the behavior of the offending party in ways that have nothing to do with you.
4. Write down how your view of the event changes if any of these five options are true.

Whenever your brain is tempted to take something personally, go through this exercise and challenge yourself to think of these depersonalized explanations—they were tired, they needed a break, they got distracted. Give your brain alternatives to consider.

For real, though. It's not about you.

When it feels personal

When you're taking something personally, it's good to understand why. Ask yourself the following three questions to uncover more about what is going on inside your head in a given situation:

1. **Why am I finding this so upsetting?** What about this is really bothering me? What are my thoughts telling me?
2. **What am I making this mean?** Are my thoughts about this situation telling me something negative about myself in some way? Are they telling me I'm not valuable enough, good enough, etc.?
3. **When did I feel like this in the past?** Is there a past trauma being triggered by this event? What past pain or hurt comes to mind when I think of my life or experiences?

TAKEAWAYS

- Nothing other people say or do is personal.
- Even when it feels personal, whatever someone does or says reflects what they have going on inside of them, not you.
- When you take things personally, you forget other people are acting "for" themselves, not "against" you.
- To help you take things less personally, consider alternate, non-personal motivations behind the offender's behavior.

Journal prompt: How would I show up differently if I took nothing personally?

CHAPTER 14

"WHO AM I?"

Confirmation bias

Ever wonder why your brain shows up with evidence to make you feel worse when you're already feeling down, defeated, deflated, or discouraged?

Let's say you bombed a live TV news appearance, and you're sitting in your car crying with frustration because you fumbled your words and lost your train of thought halfway through your sentence. At this precise moment of intensive vulnerability, your brain conveniently begins to play the crash-and-burn highlight reel of your life. That time you screwed up a presentation at work. The time in grade school when you froze in front of the whole class while presenting your project. And 10 others. The soundtrack of this delightful mental movie is something like, *See, I told you. You aren't cut out for this. You don't have what it takes. You were delusional to think you could be good at something like this.* Can you tell I'm speaking from experience?

An all-star of selective memory, your brain is actively choosing which "evidence" to present, proving your inadequacy. This phenomenon is known as confirmation bias. Something happens (interview goes terribly), you have thoughts about it (*I can't believe I did that—I'm such a failure*), and then your brain rummages through your subconscious filing cabinet and finds a slew of similar scenarios from your past, aiming to confirm the thought (personalized fail video featuring your entire life).

You might be thinking, *But, Julia, all those things did happen in the past. So doesn't that prove I can't do anything right?* Short answer: Nope! While those events did happen, your brain on confirmation bias is selectively remembering your screw-ups only. At the same time, your brain is selectively forgetting all the times you did well, everything turned out fine, and your efforts were a success. What about those times? Your brain so badly likes to be right that it will block out a whole category of experiences: aka the "every time I won" folder. Lucky for you, now you know the gig is up.

Negativity bias

In all human brains there is also something called "negativity bias," which was discovered by psychologists Paul Rozin and Edward Royzman. Their research noted the brain's tendency is to not only focus on the bad more than the good, but also to dwell on it. Left unmanaged, your brain will automatically default to negative thoughts about the bad of the past, the present, and even the future. Your brain's default setting is to concentrate on what makes you inadequate, unworthy, or unlovable. Getting your brain into a neutral, let alone positive, state is not for the faint of heart.

Rozin and Royzman's research suggests negativity bias was originally meant for our self-preservation. If you went walking around the wilderness on a sunny afternoon, expecting you were safe, you wouldn't have your wits about you to listen for predators, monitor the weather, or any number of horrifying things that could harm you. Prehistoric humans needed to be aware of the potential for danger to stay alive. Although this is still true in certain circumstances, we are no longer watching out for lions or stampedes of elephants on a daily basis. Instead, we're dealing with embarrassing moments in meetings, frets over someone not answering an email, or our boss looking at us funny. *All* of these things cause our negativity bias to kick in, forcing us to dwell on all the bad things that may come. Our brains simply haven't caught up with the times and therefore magnify non-threats like messing up an interview as if that failure is threatening your life. Your brain believes it is preserving your life by no-showing for the interview; however, it's taking away from it. This leaves you with the belief your life is only difficult, disappointing, and painful.

What both negativity bias and confirmation bias fail to recognize is the conflicting experiences and positive memories stowed safely away in your brain files. And it's your job, as your own conscious mind manager, to intentionally recall them and play the mental movie for yourself. Between your painful memories lie stories of trust, love, joy, celebration, safety, and success. While these shouldn't replace your painful memories, as those can be useful on occasion, they will hopefully balance your mind so you can create a complete story. One that includes both the stories of struggles and those of your redemption.

Devil's advocate

Several years ago, I attended a week-long intensive training with internationally renowned Cognitive Behavioral Therapy expert David Burns. (If you want to get *me* starstruck, show me a human psychology researcher!) During one of the sessions, Dr Burns asked for a volunteer. My desire to be up close and personal with one of the greatest minds of our time immediately overtook my dread of public display, and my sweaty palm shot up in the air. As a girl who was never picked first for anything, when he called me up on stage in front of 100 other therapists, my mixed feelings of terror and redemption were at an all-time high.

He proceeded to guide me through an exercise called "Devil's Advocate." He started by asking me to recall a recent situation during which I'd felt terrible. With Dr Burns and the rest of the crowded banquet hall watching intensely, I shared how I'd recently gone on a camping trip with my husband and sister, as well as my best friend, her husband, and her sister. During the trip, my best friend and her sister went off several times together without extending invitations to the rest of us (i.e. me), and it'd been bothering me ever since.

"Okay," he replied. "So, why are you still thinking about this? Why is this still bothering you several weeks later? What did her going off with her sister mean about you?"

"Well," I replied tentatively, my stomach flipping like a pancake, "maybe that she doesn't value me as much as I do her. And maybe that I'm not lovable at all."

Although this was emotionally wrenching enough, the exercise was far from over. He said the exercise was going to proceed with him posing as a sort of Devil Julia who was going to narrate all the critical, mean-hearted, nasty words I may be thinking pertaining to my lovability. My job, as non-Devil Julia, was to stand up for myself and "win" the argument against him.

I took the deepest breath I had in weeks, attempting to mentally prepare myself. The exchange went something like this:

Dr Burns as Devil Julia: Hey, Julia, your friend there, she didn't spend that much time with you on your trip. That must mean she doesn't really like you, right?

Me: Just because she wanted to spend time with her sister doesn't mean she doesn't care about me. We've been friends for years. I know she loves me.

Devil Julia: Well, this isn't the first time someone has chosen to spend time with someone else over you, is it?

Me: I don't have to be the center of everyone's world to be a valuable human being. My friends aren't always the center of my world. I like to spend time with a variety of people, too.

Devil Julia: Maybe so, but if she liked you more, she'd still choose you over anyone else to spend time with. Or at least she'd invite you to join them.

Me (advocating for myself with greater depth now): My friend not spending every minute with me on our trip doesn't mean I'm not worthy or valuable. Even if it *was* that she didn't want to spend time with me or our friendship doesn't mean much to her, it's still not an objective evaluation of my worth. My worthiness is not determined by anyone else. I AM LOVABLE AND I AM WORTHY BECAUSE I AM HERE ON THIS PLANET, AND MY EXISTENCE IS THE ONLY PREREQUISITE FOR MY WORTHINESS!

This may or may not have been followed by a bout of public, soul-cleansing tears. In that moment, I felt the years I'd been plagued by unworthiness begin to heal. David as Devil Julia— taking the role of my voice telling me I wasn't enough—had finally pushed me to fight for my right to exist. That is the power of thought. Mine, yours, ours. Our thoughts change our lives.

EXERCISE: WHO AM I?

This exercise is designed to help you build your relationship with yourself. In any healthy relationship, the more you get to know someone, the more you understand, are connected to, and deeply value them. This isn't any different when it comes to your relationship with yourself, although we rarely take the time to truly get to know ourselves (but then wonder why we feel emotionally unstable). Today, you're going to stop that cycle. Take a few moments now to get to know yourself a little better using the questions below. The dividends returned on this investment are worth it. Trust me, the person who cried in front of my version of a celebrity god and 100 of his followers.

1. *What do I like/dislike?*

    What foods do you like? What topics interest you? What kinds of people are you drawn to? What experiences do you enjoy? Do you like to be around other people or by yourself? Do you like to be active with your body, your mind, or both? Do you like deep conversation or solitary reflection? List as many things as you can. When you're done, do the same for your dislikes—sometimes these are much clearer. What triggers you? What makes your blood boil? What repels you? Ideals you can't get behind? Pet peeves? Make it comprehensive.

2. *What's important to me?*

    What matters to you? Or who? How do you want to help the world and make a difference? Is there something you're involved in or would like to be? Dig deep with your values and beliefs across a wide variety of areas (i.e., religious, political, interpersonal, social, etc.).

3. *What's easy/hard for me?*

    You may not often notice what you find easy. Take time to think about what happens without you having to think much about it—something that might not come as easily to everyone. Are you an excellent speaker? Writer? A natural athlete? A creative crafter? Would you be a professional student if you could? Do you always find yourself teaching others? Are your hands magic? Is your mind agile? Can you tune into other people's emotions like they're a radio station? Are you a born leader? An excellent follower? Once you've listed everything you're amazing at, go opposite. What's hard for you? Where do you struggle a bit more than others? Don't forget this is an information-seeking, not a critical, activity. Stay neutral.

4. *What lights me up?*
I love exploring this question; it's brilliant (pun intended). So, what is it for you? Is it connection, reading, music, people, places, art, moving your body, or resting? What excites you and brings you joy? What makes you feel connected and alive? List it all.

Take your time and write down your thoughts on these questions in your journal. Explore all these questions over the next couple of weeks and, perhaps most importantly, enjoy it. You should know who you really are.

TAKEAWAYS

- Just because you have a thought doesn't mean it's true. Your thoughts are not even originally yours in many cases.
- Make sure you take the time to fairly represent your past experiences in your memory slideshow—don't focus on the negative ones only.
- The next time your brain is making you feel terrible, talk back to your carful of inner critics and show them who's boss.
- Building your relationship with yourself is as important as building your relationships with others.

Journal prompt: What self-critical thoughts have been sitting in the front seat of my brain for too long? What would happen if I kicked them out?

CHAPTER 15

"I'M NOT GOOD ENOUGH"

Serious question: How would you know if you were good enough? Take a minute or two to think about it.

Now, we're going to check back in with our primitive brains for a moment. Remember how our fear of judgment is a survival instinct? A long time ago, when we lived in tribes, fully dependent on one another for our survival, we couldn't risk being kicked out of our clans. Being sent out into the wilderness to fend for ourselves was a recipe for almost certain death. So, likeability and helpfulness were key traits that allowed our ancestors to fit in with their tribes and survive. And while these traits are still valued in modern society, it would be a disservice not to call out the obvious imbalance of how important these traits continue to be, depending upon your gender.

For centuries upon centuries, women have been socialized to derive their value from what they can do for others. Brought up to believe their role as helper, healer, and nurturer is how their worth is attained. Being kind and compassionate is a beautiful thing, of course. But when generosity comes at the cost of one's own wellbeing, it's not quite as lovely as it sounds.

In her book *Untamed*, Glennon Doyle discusses how society has collectively agreed that the epitome of a valuable, admirable, and noteworthy woman is one who is selfless.

Essentially, a woman who has lost herself for the sake of others is the aspiration. The woman with no sense of self is the ideal. Well, it's no wonder girls grow up thinking it's their responsibility to make others happy at the expense of losing themselves. If you're told for long enough that everyone else should be taken care of without considering your own wants or needs, it's bound to make an impression.

To be fair, men who feel this sense of over-responsibility to the point of self-neglect exist. However, women have been largely socialized this way as a gender. I've seen many couples come across my couch whose relationship dynamic makes this apparent. The husband who announces he'll be on the golf course all day Saturday, thinking little of leaving his wife at home with the house, kids, and chores. His wife, on the other hand, asks permission to have a two-hour dinner with a friend. And if permission is given, she will spend a good part of the day cooking, prepping, and planning the evening so there's as little as possible for him to be responsible for while he's home holding the fort down. This dichotomy is present even in many modern relationships, with no one thinking there's anything off-balance. But the question is, how are you supposed to feel good enough if you're only valued based on what you do for others or what you give up for yourself?

More on self-acceptance

What if who you are right now, in this moment, is already good enough? If you're going to value yourself for who you are, it also means you have to be who you are. It's nice to feel good about yourself, but being yourself without apology is next level. How often do you muse about everything you've yet to accomplish, acquire, change, improve, or become before you can feel good enough?

I was self-conscious about my body for a long time, partially because my thick legs were referred to as "thunder thighs" or "elephant stumps" from the time I was 11 years old. At some point, I learned to believe there was something inferior about my body, which translated into there being something inferior about *me*. (Don't even get me started on how other than selflessness, women are expected to meet a specific—yet ever-changing—socially prescribed waist-to-hip ratio.)

I grew up breathing in diet and beauty industry propaganda in the 90s, and I believed the only way I could be worthy was to find a way to have thin, long, smooth, curveless Kate Moss legs. And, boy, did I try. This followed me until just a few years ago, when I saw women showing up, comfortable, confident, and authentic on social media with all different body shapes, sizes, compositions, and colors.

This may sound weird, but until then I didn't know I was allowed to do that. I didn't know I could love and accept my body for exactly what it was. I didn't know my physique didn't have to look like the women in the magazines before I could feel good.

I want to make sure I explicitly say that self-acceptance applies to every aspect of you. Every single one. When Shame says you're not good enough and you need to be something or someone else first, Worthiness says you are enough as you are. Your worth is not dependent on anyone or anything else outside of you; it's already there waiting to be acknowledged.

Accepting yourself for who you are doesn't mean never working on yourself. Maybe you want to be more patient, less judgmental, more compassionate, have better boundaries, or reach an important goal. Self-acceptance says, though, you're not doing these things to *become* a better, more worthy person; you're doing them because you want to *have* better in your life. You want to have better relationships with both others and yourself, and you want to have more rich and rewarding experiences in your life. You also want to *feel* better. You want to learn, grow, experience, experiment, and expand in this short time you're here on this earth. You aren't making changes to earn your worth; you're getting in the driver's seat of your life and experiencing your worth.

Mind reading

How often do you assume you know what someone else is thinking? Have you ever gotten a sideways glance mid-meeting from a colleague and thought they were judging you? Or believed when a friend didn't text you back right away it was on purpose? Have you ever devoted an entire day reviewing something over and over wondering what someone meant when they said x? If you're anything like me and the rest of the humans, it doesn't feel great to assume everyone is thinking the worst about you.

What if, just for fun, you replayed some of your mind-reading scenarios and assumed people were thinking the best about you? You don't actually know for sure what they were thinking, so if you're going to have a thought about their thoughts anyways, why not choose a thought that feels good? I mean, you do have that option.

When I started to choose thoughts assuming people were thinking well of me, so much changed. I felt lighter and I showed up with more vigor. I encourage you to try it. Instead of assuming the mid-meeting side-eye was judgmental, assume they thought your idea was kind of brilliant. Replace the anxiety of someone ignoring you with the assumption your friend got distracted and forgot. You don't have an obligation to fuel the worst-case scenario, especially since the best-case scenario makes for a much better day-to-day experience.

Being real

In the words of American actor Sanford Meisner, "That which hinders your task is your task." When I first heard this quote, I didn't get it. However, when I was finally able to wrap my brain around it, something important shifted inside me. Take a moment with it: "That which hinders your task is your task."

Many humans think our imperfections are getting in our way, so the solution is to be more perfect. More success, accomplishments, stability, control, discipline—and the list goes on. If we finish our to-do list, then we will be happy, and then we'll like ourselves. But when you break down Meisner's words, he's saying the opposite is true. You don't need to be more perfect to feel good enough. In fact, that is what's hindering you and your task of feeling good enough. So your task, should you choose to accept it, is to work on loving yourself with your imperfections instead of making perfection the prerequisite.

Isn't it funny how often we fall into this perfection-seeking thought trap? I know I've been there. And although you may think your have-it-all-together-and-is-on-top-of-it-all mask will make you look sparkly and new so others will be drawn to you, perfecting and performing actually keeps genuine human connection at bay. The more you put on a front, the less other not-perfect-either-because-no-one-is humans will be able to relate to you.

I'm sure you don't connect to perfect, so why would someone else? Sure, it's easy to admire those people who seem to live the ultimate calm and collected lives, with their curated feed of home décor, neverending success, model discipline, and flawless wardrobe, but do you feel like you ever truly connect to those people? Probably not, unless you're close enough with them to know they don't actually have it together either.

The belief that people are going to like you more if you're perfect is a backward, big, fat lie. If you like people more when you see their messy, vulnerable, imperfect side, it's safe to say they'll like the same from you. Also, have you ever felt uncomfortable opening up to a person who doesn't seem to understand what a messy life is? I know I have. So, while being honest and vulnerable can be scary at first, I've found in practice that it leads to deeper, more meaningful connections because, frankly, none of us lead mess-free lives.

EXERCISE: LESS PLEASING, PERFECTING, AND PERFORMING

Take a moment to ask yourself the following:

1. Who are you trying to please in your life, and why? What do you think you'll get if you succeed and what is it costing you while you try?
2. What are you trying to perfect in your life, and why? What do you think you'll get if you succeed and what is it costing you while you try?
3. Where are you trying to overperform in your life, and why? What do you think you'll get if you succeed and what is it costing you when you try?

Write your answers down. They're important.

Fear

A few years ago, I decided something. It was time for me to share my knowledge with more than my individual clients. Not everyone has the means to afford a therapist, and I thought if I could share some of the tools I was using with my clients in online videos, it would make mind management and healing accessible to more than the privileged. A few YouTube videos in, I serendipitously heard about the live streaming app, Periscope. At the time, my first two children were under two years old, so teaching and connecting with other adults was the social interaction I'd been missing.

There was a problem, though. I loved this idea, but my perfectionist brain was terrified. For the first several—okay, fine, for the first 100 plus—live mental wellness talks I did, my finger would shake uncontrollably as I pushed the Go Live button. How do I know it was my perfectionist brain causing the drama? Like clockwork, after every 6–10-minute talk, my brain would default to picking apart and scrutinizing every little detail. *You didn't make x point more clearly. You forgot to say y. You talked too fast/too slow, and you said "sort of" too much.* Of course, it's not bad to improve your skills, but not at the cost of being terrible to yourself every step of the way.

After many, many shaky-fingered lives followed by mental berating, I heard the question loud and clear, "But what about having the courage to be imperfect, Julia?" The words stung, even if they were only in my mind. I was teaching it, but not living it. So I finally decided it was high time to tap into my bravery and run directly toward my imperfections instead of running away from them.

Contrary to popular belief, being brave is not the presence of complete confidence, nor is it the absence of fear. Bravery is when you feel vulnerable, exposed, and uncertain, but you do what you set out to do anyway. Bravery is speaking up about injustice, setting a clear boundary, having a tough conversation, or showing up and letting your imperfect self be seen. Being brave is when you decide fear won't hold you back or keep you quiet. In fact, bravery often brings fear along for the ride. Fear is there, but Bravery is in the driver's seat.

Building self-esteem

Spoiler alert: Trying to change yourself on your outside in order to change something on your inside is a losing battle. You can't heal a deep wound by changing your looks, relationship, or job. You can't mend your pain with success and approval. Building self-esteem is an inside job and no matter where you go, that's where you are. You can't outrun, out-please, out-perfect, or out-perform your way into a solid relationship with yourself. But you can be kind.

EXERCISE: YOUR SELF-ESTEEM SCORE

Are you in the driver's seat of your self-esteem? Score one point for every question you can confidently answer with a "True".

1. You try things that interest you without checking with others first for approval.
2. You allow yourself to be imperfect.
3. You don't "fish" for compliments.
4. You're not overly nice to gain the favor of other people.
5. You don't review your emails multiple times to ensure they're perfect before you hit send.
6. You know if someone doesn't like your choices, that doesn't always mean you're wrong.
7. You don't beat yourself up when you make mistakes.
8. You don't lie in bed at night worrying about what people think about you.
9. You don't spend a lot of time trying to become someone else.
10. You can celebrate other people's achievements.
11. You can celebrate your own achievements—big OR small.
12. You're okay spending some time alone.
13. You're able to be flexible when changes happen.
14. You don't take things personally very often.
15. You believe you are worthy of a good life, love, and success.
16. You trust in your ability to adapt to change.
17. You're not threatened by disagreements with others.
18. You don't compare yourself to others too often.
19. You're okay if not everyone likes you.
20. You don't try to make everyone like you.

If you scored:

15–20 Look at you! Good job! Your relationship with yourself seems to be going well.

10–15 Don't despair, but you may need to reconnect with yourself. You're worth it.

0–10 Hey, friend, you're in need of some self-love and self-compassion! Never forget you are worthy, no one is perfect, and definitely no one has it all figured out.

Nathaniel Branden has been coined the father of self-esteem after writing his bestselling *The Six Pillars of Self-Esteem*. Through his research, he found that our self-esteem can be broken into two parts: self-efficacy and self-respect. Self-efficacy is your belief in your ability to be successful in the things you set out to do. It's confidence that you have at least some control over your motivation, behavior, and your social environment. It's the knowledge that although you might not have control over your circumstances, you always have choices within them.

Self-respect, on the other hand, is about value. It's answering the questions: How much do you value yourself? How connected are you to your inherent sense of worthiness? Do you believe you deserve to be happy and have a good life? Do you understand your value in just being yourself? How often do you pay attention to yourself and value your wants, needs, preferences, and perspectives? Are you directing your own life and your own choices? If you want a solid relationship with yourself, respecting yourself is a must at the foundation of your relationship (just as it is with any healthy relationship).

I was out on a lunch date with myself a little while ago when I had a profound realization. I realized that I liked myself. I mean, I really liked myself. I liked the thoughts going through my head while I ate my chicken noodle soup and accompanying sourdough bun. I liked being with myself and was thoroughly enjoying my own company. After years of a tumultuous relationship with myself in which I often felt terrible about who I was, to sit and just enjoy me was a liberating thing.

Your true, life partner

You are the only person you are absolutely guaranteed to live with every moment from birth until death, so if you're not working on that relationship every single day, it's time to start. If you're not quite sure how, let me assure you, it's easier than you think. Think about a relationship in your life you would describe as strong, safe, and trusting. Now, think about all the things that make this relationship so. What does that person do or say to make you feel good about being with them? How do they talk to you? Do they put you down and constantly highlight all your flaws and weaknesses? Or are they encouraging, caring, and supportive? Do they minimize your successes? Or do they celebrate you and acknowledge you for even the small steps in the right direction? And when you answer these questions, that is your answer to how to work on your self-relationship.

Your relationship with yourself matters, but funnily enough, it's often the one you tend to last. Time spent in your outside relationships is time well spent, but you also need to find strength, love, and care within. Your sense of self is the foundation of everything you do, so when you're not feeling good about yourself, life doesn't feel good.

When self-relationships are neglected, humans cope in three common ways: shutting down, over-pleasing/performing/perfecting, or feeling shame followed by avoidance. In contrast, when humans are secure and solid in who they are, they show up differently—better, I daresay. When you're not constantly fighting with Shame for the wheel, you're bound to be more present, patient, connected, respectful, and effective. Therefore, working on your relationship with you not only feels better, but it also makes the world a better place.

TAKEAWAYS

- Be real. Other people will like you more and so will you (which is the important part).
- Instead of assuming people are thinking the worst, try assuming they're thinking the best.
- Building your self-esteem is an inside job. It's created through building a solid self-relationship founded on how you treat yourself.
- You live with yourself from day one until the end, so investing in yourself is worth it.

Journal prompt: When I am feeling more secure and confident in who I am, what do I notice myself thinking? What would happen if I practiced thinking those thoughts more?

CHAPTER 16

"I'M A FAILURE"

"I'm a failure."

This statement commonly serves two purposes: 1) To make yourself feel terrible and 2) To stop you from trying new, interesting, rewarding, or beautiful things because you don't want to feel terrible again. In a nutshell: it's a totally useless statement—unless you like feeling bad and holding yourself back.

"Don't do it!" says your mind. "Don't take a risk and apply for that new job—do you really want to feel this way again if you're not hired for the position? Or, worse, if you're not even chosen for an interview?"

"Don't start the business," your brain says with an eye-roll (yes, in this scenario your brain has eyes). "Most small businesses fail, so yours probably will too. Does setting yourself up for failure sound like a good use of your time?"

"Don't ask that seemingly stable, gorgeous, lovely human out on a date," nags the voice in your head. "They'll probably say no. Is that the kind of rejection you're looking for on a Friday?"

Although the part of your brain that's trying to protect you from pain seems like it has great intentions, your fear of experiencing even a little bit of temporary emotional discomfort (which you now know from reading this book is actually much less threatening) happens to be preventing you from living your rich and meaningful life. How many things aren't you doing right now because your fear of failure won your internal debate? Fear, in its own way, was attempting to keep you safe, but is not achieving everything you set out to do actually unsafe? For the most part, the answer is no. It's just experiencing an outcome you didn't want, which probably doesn't equate world-ending catastrophe. To help redirect your brain when it's preventing you from fully living your life, keep these statements accessible:

- "Thank you for trying to make me safe, but this is not a dangerous or unsafe situation. If it doesn't go the way I want it to, it might be uncomfortable, but I can get through it and I am willing to take that risk."
- "Thank you for trying to keep me safe, but I've got this. I can handle whatever happens."
- "Things don't have to go my way for me to be okay. I will be okay no matter the outcome."
- "I can do hard things. I have before and I will again."
- "I've come this far and I am not going to quit now."
- "I am passionate about this and I am going to pursue it further even if everything doesn't go exactly how I want it to."

This doesn't mean you won't be shaking in your booties when you step into the arena of life, but your fear of a less-than-ideal outcome isn't going to stop you from doing so. Remember, courage isn't action in the absence of fear; it's taking action while fear comes along for the ride.

Failure and your inner critic

Failure is truly insidious. It joins forces with your inner critic and works hard to convince you that your failures, rather than your successes, represent you. The last time you experienced failure, what did you tell yourself? Was it, "Urgh! That didn't go the way I wanted it to. Welp, guess it was quite the failure"? Or did your self-talk trend more toward, "Urgh! That didn't go the way I wanted it to. Welp, guess *I'm* quite the failure"? The key word difference here is *it* vs. *I*. Depending on how you phrase it, the result might mean something about your identity instead of just describing an event that happened. Not everything you set out to do is going to go your way. That's life.

You get to choose what failure means to you. If you go with neutrality, failure is simply a result you didn't desire or expect. Your thoughts are what determine how you feel about it. You could spiral out and make a failure mean you're incapable, not good enough, and whatever other kick-yourself-while-you're-down messages are your go-to. You could also change your default thoughts and make failure mean you have more to learn, and will now look to see how you could do things differently next time. You could also recognize your attempt at something as a reflection of your courage, instead of letting the outcome be the sole determinant of your emotional experience

In and of itself, failure doesn't mean anything. There's no need to give it enough credence to make you feel terrible about yourself, or stop you from trying again. Your outcomes aren't always your choice, but how you choose to think about them absolutely is. As with every attempt, you'll either get the outcome you want or the lesson you need.

EXERCISE: TAKE A SUCCESS INVENTORY

Whenever you say to yourself, "I'm a failure," you're inviting confirmation bias to show up with every supporting example from your past that proves this hypothesis is correct: "Remember that time you failed that exam?" or, "Remember when you worked really hard on that proposal and it fell flat?" or, "Remember when you planned that party and hardly anyone showed up?" *Failure. Failure. Failure.*

But that's not how evidence works. Hypotheses aren't proven true by exclusively reporting supporting data. In fact, there's a name for that: cherry-picking, and it's an unacceptable way to prove your point. Instead, all evidence must be considered, so you're going to take a success inventory. To balance out your self-sabotaging thoughts, your assignment is to sit down and make a 20-item list of your successes—small and large alike. That time you got an A on your grade school spelling test? Write it down. When your friend told you how insightful you are after helping them work through a personal issue? Add it to the list. When you scored the winning point for your team? Excellent example. That raving annual review you received from your boss last year? Log it in glorious detail. When I made my list, the time I won the *slow* bike race during Sports Day in grade five was right there at the top. You know why? I'm still proud about it. Slow biking is no joke—do you know what kind of balancing skills that takes?

If you can make it higher than 20, fantastic. List as many times you can think of when you've been resourceful, helpful, perseverant, strong, or creative. Add them to your inventory and pay attention to how you feel. Who's the failure now? Not you, that's for sure.

How to be bouncy

Think about someone who doesn't let failure faze them— someone who will not be held back or kept down, even when they are unsuccessful. Do you get yourself back up after you've fallen? Do you know how?

Everyone falls, but your quality of life is not determined by your falls, but by whether you get back up. You don't have to get back up right away, but you do have to get back up if you want to keep going, growing, and flowing. Upon receiving not my first, but my second, rejection letter after dedicating two and a half years to building a strong application for graduate school (this was on top of my four and a half years spent completing my bachelor's degree), I literally collapsed on the ground wailing, "Whyyyy!!! This is so not faaaaiiiirrr!!! Why do I suck so muuuuchhh?!" However, after a slightly embarrassing amount of time, I picked myself up, had a stern talk with myself, and decided I wasn't going to trash my dream of becoming a therapist just because of two lousy rejection letters. And I hit the books again the next day.

Dr Martin Seligman, the creator of Positive Psychology, found that people who learn resilience are happier, more successful, and have more fulfilling lives. Do you know why? The answer isn't because they're constantly successful. It's because they know how to persevere when they fail, so they're not afraid of it. They try more things, put themselves out there, and take (reasonable) risks. They build more, they create more, they try more, and they love more. And as a result, they experience a richer and more fulfilling life than those who let fear drive.

Merriam-Webster defines resilience as *an ability to recover from or adjust easily to misfortune or change*. Resilience isn't just about sucking it up as quickly as possible. Resilience requires emotional intelligence, which means taking the time to process the failure, setback, or undesirable outcome.

When you're knocked down, start with reflection about how you're feeling and where you feel it. Then, show yourself compassion and understanding. It's understandable you're discouraged, because you worked hard. It makes sense that you're disappointed, because you really wanted them to say yes. You were sure you had it this time, so it's no surprise you're feeling defeated. In these moments, put your inner critic in the backseat and invite your kinder inner voice to the front—the voice of the unwaveringly understanding friend who's always there when you need them.

After you've shown yourself compassion for your feelings, take a step back and give yourself credit where credit is due. You may have failed, but you put yourself out there and tried something hard. You may have been hurt, but you opened yourself up and let yourself love someone. Trying big things and going for what you really want takes guts. It takes courage and strength to try and fail, especially when you don't know exactly how it's all going to turn out.

When you practice resilience, you can take lessons from the failure. What did you learn about what doesn't work? What did you learn about potential strategies? What did you learn about what you don't want? What did you learn about yourself?

Then pull yourself back up and try again.

TAKEAWAYS

- You are going to fail sometimes. Failure is inevitable, so you might as well try.
- Failing is a good way to learn and grow.
- Work on failing well—process your feelings, offer yourself compassion, give yourself credit where it's due, find the lesson, and then get back up.

Journal prompt: What would I do differently if I decided failing wasn't a big deal?

CHAPTER 17

"I WILL BE HAPPY WHEN I ..."

We love waiting for life to get good. We love the anticipation of believing life will finally be good when [insert specific happiness marker here]. When we finally reach a certain level of professional success, have x dollars in savings, find the ideal partner, have raised our children to be independent, are thinner or stronger, achieve inbox zero, clean and organize our home, have full emotional control in every (previously triggering) interaction—the list of our Tomorrow-Me fantasies is endless. We tell ourselves, "My life will be complete and I'll finally feel satisfied when I achieve, acquire, arrive at, or complete..." Right? Wrong.

Although some hope is positive, as it gives us something to look forward to and work toward, it's not so good when the anticipation of a better tomorrow is our primary focus. We then forget to connect with the goodness of our present. As appealing as it may be, we will never experience the future. Forever, our experience is the here and now. Today, at some point in the past, was our anticipated future. That's right. Read it again if you need to.

If we can't find joy in the present moment, we won't find it in the future. At one point in your life, you were hoping for much of what you have right now. It's time to be grateful for (and take the time to want) what you have instead of spending time waiting for the next thing you don't. If you can't be happy now, in the place where you once wished to be, when *will* you be?

You see, happiness is not a destination; it's a discipline. Happiness is choosing what's in front of you and engaging in the joy available to you at any given time. It's pausing to appreciate where you are and what you have. Don't mistake this for toxic positivity. I'm not saying if you're in the middle of a crisis you should just think positive and everything will be better. However, when you show deep gratitude for your current self and life as a rule, the cultural messages we're fed about happiness waiting around the corner become less appealing. Where you are now used to be a dream. Live in it.

Living your dream life

Think about the things you've already accomplished on your "What I Need to Be Happy" list. Are you happy yet? In many ways, you're currently living the life of your dreams. There was a time you thought finally finishing school and having more freedom was the solution to your woes. You thought making better money would be your ticket to happiness. You were determined finding your perfect match would set you up for a life of joy and bliss. You believed starting a family would surely satiate your deepest desire. Or getting that promotion. Or getting the kids out of the house. Or getting fit. Or taking that dream vacation. Or renovating the kitchen. Or having less on your to-do list. Or, or, or, or, or…

I remember being an angsty, aching-for-independence 14-year-old who dreamt of her 16th birthday daily. Then, she could finally get her driver's license and drive her friends to 7Eleven for Slurpees anytime she wanted. Turning 16 was going to be the solution to all my problems. It was going to set me up for my dream life of cruising down the suburban strip with my posse and blasting Lauryn Hill, our cold treats sloshing around while singing "Killing Me Softly" at the top of our lungs. When

I think about it, I have been technically living my dream life for over 20 years now. What the heck do I have to complain about?

EXERCISE: WANTING WHAT YOU ALREADY HAVE

Time to make another list. For this one, write down 20 things you really wanted at any point in your life that you now have. If you have more than 20, you go! This should help you connect deeply with the ways your present is what you've always wanted and give your brain a break from waiting for the future. Come on, what have you accomplished that was once a wisp of a dream?

Being present

Even though much of your current reality is the embodiment of many things you were once waiting for, it's normal to forget to notice. When our human brains aren't looking for ways to justify our negative bias, they have a hard time staying with the now due to being focused on what's next. It takes ongoing practice to be more present with what is and find the joy. If you're a go-getter, don't worry, appreciating the present isn't the same as checking out of life while bingeing Netflix and pizza (although that could be a great way to spend a rainy Saturday afternoon).

We human beings are wired for growth, remember? We do best when we're learning, growing, creating, expanding, experiencing, and experimenting (with times for rest and rejuvenation in between). But when we're only focused on a future outcome without ever enjoying the present process, that's not good either. Your drive to learn, grow, expand, move forward, achieve, and accomplish is a worthy one. But there's no need to labor under the illusion of making it to a certain life level that will magically make your problems disappear. That destination doesn't exist (trust me, I've looked hard for it). Like any other feeling, happiness is created by your thoughts. You can choose it, or you can choose to dwell on your wants—so choose well.

TAKEAWAYS

- Don't spend your time waiting for the future to feel happy and successful. Decide to let yourself be happy and connected to the joy in your life exactly as it is today.
- Look for the dreams you've had that have already come true in your life. Contemplate your strengths, skills, abilities, and freedoms.
- Much of your happiness will come from learning, growing, experiencing, and expanding, but that doesn't mean you shouldn't be present in your current iteration of success and happiness.

Journal prompt: What takes me away from being present, grounded, and appreciative of where I am in my life? What allows me to be more present, grounded, and appreciative of where I am in my life?

PART FOUR

BECOME THE DRIVER OF YOUR OWN BEHAVIORS

If you always do what you've always done, then you'll always get what you've always got, and if you always get what you've got, then there ain't no change.

— Henry Ford

Perhaps you've heard this quote before. It always makes me think of the colloquial definition of insanity: repeating the same thing over and over again and expecting a different result. Isn't it funny how we all do this so often and are genuinely surprised when our results stay the same?

I'm obviously (I hope) not implying you're insane. In fact, there's a good reason you're having a hard time changing your behaviors. Any guess as to why? It's because you haven't changed your thoughts. Think back to the ABCBO model in Part One. Your thoughts create your feelings, your feelings drive your behaviors, and behaviors impact your outcomes. If your plan is to change a behavior without working on the thought two layers back, it creates what we psychology nerds call *cognitive dissonance*. Cognitive dissonance happens when your actions don't match your thoughts, which leads to a discrepancy that eventually creates an uncomfortable tension in your brain. This tension is often only broken when you revert your action back to match the original thought.

For example, let's say you want to start working out. You tell yourself you're going to work out for three 45-minute sessions weekly. At first, you're excited to get stronger and increase your energy levels. You can't wait to feel healthy and run around with your kids without getting winded. Two weeks into your new, life-changing plan, the fantasy of how great life will be when you're fit begins to wear off. At this juncture, you reduce your exercise to nothing and cancel your gym membership (or keep paying it under the promise to yourself that you'll get back at it really soon). Sound about right?

If so, it's likely somewhere in your brain lies a belief about yourself that doesn't match up with the new treadmill-running you. Maybe the belief manifests as an excuse like, *I can't keep this up, it's going to be too hard*, or, *I don't have time for this; I'll kick off my health regimen when I finish this project*. If you dig a little deeper, you might find a stronger belief about you not being a person who has what it takes to lead a healthy, active lifestyle. Or maybe, deeper still, you don't believe you deserve to feel good in the first place.

Remember how much our brains dislike change? This (natural) aversion is why altering your default thoughts is going to take work. Our brains are going to be more comfortable maintaining pre-existing thoughts than accepting new ones like, *I'm going to the gym today*. So, unless you do some intentional digging and work to change your deeper thoughts, your brain is bound to default.

Maybe you want to be more productive, be more open with others, stop people-pleasing, or have better boundaries. If the part of your brain that doesn't want those things—*It's going to be too hard. I'm probably going to fail. People might reject me. I might look selfish*—thinks louder than the motivated-to-grow part does, you won't be able to get started, let alone keep it up. In the long run, it's worth it to dig a little deeper so you can finally get what you want out of your life. Change is hard, but I have faith that you can do it. Will you join me in believing in you too?

BE that you

Once I have more motivation, then I'll get myself out power-walking every day.

Once I get the promotion, then I'll slow down and be more present with my family.

Once I am more confident, then I'll be more comfortable setting boundaries and saying no.

This is how so many people think it works. When you HAVE this thing, then you'll DO that, which will lead you to BECOME whatever version of yourself. And then you wait. You wait and hope. Someday very soon you'll HAVE the motivation, HAVE the balance, HAVE the confidence. As if hoping hard and long enough is what makes change. Unfortunately for pretty much all of us, hope is not a great strategy. Hope is a desire for things to be different, but it doesn't necessarily involve doing anything to make the difference happen.

Ready for what you should do instead of, or at least in conjunction with, hope? Being the person who has the thing already. Call to the surface the parts of you that have been dormant for too long. You have everything you need inside of you right now in this moment. You have everything you need to engage with life the ways you want, you just have to get them out of the trunk. You need to BE them.

This is not faking it till you make it. Faking it is the same as changing behavior without dealing with the underlying thoughts. No, *being* the version of you who takes action and gets results lies in your thoughts. Think about it like this: What thoughts does the person who gets out of the house every day and moves their body have about themselves? And if we dig even deeper, what is their identity? More than likely, they see themselves as a person who takes care of their body and they believe they deserve to feel healthy and energetic. They love the endorphin rush and stress reduction that comes with exercise, and they see themselves as someone who values getting their heart rate up over more lethargic activities.

They are someone who moves their body based on their strongly held beliefs about themselves. Because of their internal monologue, pulling on their runners and getting out to move is a natural behavior of someone with those beliefs. They don't have to think about it because they *are* it.

Let's look at another example. I worked on this book practically every night after tucking my kids into bed for several months straight. And let me tell you, there were some nights my brain *really* didn't want to sit down and write. At all. It wanted to plop on the couch with a lager and passively consume a load of TV. Some nights the pull to be prone was almost too strong to resist. But I'd made a commitment to daily writing and I had a plan to turn it around. I'd mentally challenge myself, *Who is the Julia who wrote a book that is out there in the world helping people change their lives and take charge of their minds and emotions? Who would she be right now?* And inevitably, the answer would come to me: *Author Julia would be the woman who sits down and gets to work because she wants to help change the world, and doing so requires taking action on her goals every day.* As soon as I connected with those parts of me, the excuse-making drama queen in my brain would quiet down, and I would have no trouble getting to work. If you want the outcome bad enough, you'll rise to the occasion. If you want the outcome bad enough, the parts of you that will get results will hop right into the driver's seat.

In this section, we'll take a closer look at the ways you already are who you aim to be, and how to let those characteristics shine.

CHAPTER 18
BE THE HEALTHY BOUNDARY-SETTER

Do you have problems with boundaries? Most people will answer that no, they don't. Actually, they'll say, I have a micro-managing boss problem, an overbearing mother-in-law problem, an over-commitment problem, and an overwhelming stress problem. But boundaries? Not so much. Welp, here I am to burst your bubble yet again. All of these things are caused by a boundary-setting problem. Although you may not be aware of it, boundaries (or lack thereof) are at the root of many people's struggles. Let's see how yours are and discover how to shore them up a bit.

EXERCISE: 20 SIGNS OF UNHEALTHY BOUNDARIES

If you're unsure about whether you struggle with setting boundaries, the list below will help you figure it out. Check off all that apply to you.

1. Overworking yourself to the point of burnout.
2. Doing things you don't want to do to avoid upsetting anyone.

3. Going against your personal values or ethics to please others.
4. Getting annoyed at others for nosing into your business.
5. Getting frustrated with people who won't give you space.
6. Feeling like you're obligated to do something just because someone asked.
7. Taking on more than you can handle.
8. Feeling resentful toward others for not appreciating you.
9. Allowing people to take whatever they want from you.
10. Letting other people make decisions for you (or asking them to).
11. Defining yourself based on what others say or do.
12. Feeling uncomfortable at the thought of saying no.
13. Feeling guilty when you say no.
14. Saying yes when you want to say no.
15. Feeling angry toward others when they ask things of you.
16. Taking something on because you want people to think you're a "good" person.
17. Agreeing to do things just so that people won't reject you.
18. Thinking people won't value you unless you go along with what they want.
19. Getting angry because you never get a break.
20. Judging other people when they have boundaries.

How'd it go? If you ticked off a few of them, we've got a little boundary work to do. If you ticked off most or all of them, we've got more than a little boundary work ahead of us. Rest assured, it doesn't mean you're bad if you ticked off all of them. Most people are not taught how to have healthy boundaries. If you were never taught, how could you have them now?

What is a boundary?

Boundaries have become a bit of a buzzword in recent years, and for good reason. I, for one, first learned what a boundary was just over 10 years ago (which is not that long ago for someone who's been struggling with them her entire life). And I quickly became a believer. Setting healthy boundaries seriously changed my life and now I won't shut up about them. Their life-altering properties are exactly why they've been a hot topic in social-emotional circles and I hope they stay there.

If you have a boundary problem—which, not going to lie, you probably do—it's not only because you weren't taught how to have healthy ones, but also because most of us don't actually understand what "having boundaries" means. If you've started trying to set better boundaries but have found it more frustrating than effective, I've got some news for you. First, you are definitely not alone. And second, you're about to get a few tweaks that will help you a lot.

For starters, the most important thing to know about boundaries is also the biggest barrier to having good ones: Boundaries are not meant to change anyone else. That's right. I'm going to repeat it one more time. *Effective boundaries require little to nothing of anyone other than you.* Here's the deal: Boundaries have little to do with others because they're *your* boundaries. So, even if they are boundaries with others, they are about you deciding what is and is not okay with you, what that looks like across your relationships, and your plan if they are violated.

For example, if we were talking about your yard, you'd have rules for it—boundaries around what's acceptable and what's not in that space. Perhaps you want people to stay out of the garden or maybe people are expected to enter through a gate, not climb over your carefully constructed fence. Well, if people wanted to come and play in your yard, you'd expect them to follow the rules, right? And if they chose not to follow the rules—especially more than once—then it's probably fair to say they wouldn't be welcome in your yard anymore, and you'd let them know it. Anyone is allowed to think gardens are meant to be trampled through and, frankly, they can do that in their own if they want to; they're just not allowed to do so in yours. Imagine if you kept similar rules in place for your life?

Essentially, boundaries are all about what you will or will not do, and what you will or will not tolerate. A boundary is an assertion of my choice based on your choice. You choose to yell at me? I will choose to disengage from the conversation if or until you can speak to me in a moderate tone. You choose to make passive-aggressive remarks when we're together? I will choose to spend less time with you until you're willing to have an honest conversation about what's bothering you. You choose to come home drunk? I will choose to take the kids and stay at my parents' place. You choose to show up late for our coffee date? I will choose to leave when I originally planned to make my yoga class. You choose not to commit to weekend plans? I choose to make plans with someone else. If you're not used to boundaries, this may sound like a list of ultimatums. It's not. We are both making choices. And sometimes my choice is affected by your choice, depending on what is best and healthy for me.

You can request any change you want in a relationship, and the person(s) affected gets to decide whether they will acquiesce. It's the beauty of free will in action. If they choose not to accept the boundary you set, it's your choice to follow through on your boundary or not. (Hint: the follow-through might just be the most important—albeit the most difficult—part.)

Boundaries, in most cases, do not require others to be a certain way so you can be okay. No, we are okay no matter what because we know what we expect of others and ourselves. Remember, when you base your happiness and wellbeing on how someone else behaves, they are in charge of how you feel instead of you, which is not an ideal situation. But when each person functions based on their own ABCBO model—behaving based on their feelings, which are driven by their thoughts—life becomes a lot easier.

When our actions are about ourselves and no one else, we can also begin to internalize that other people's actions aren't about us. I'm not saying following through on our boundaries is easy. It can be rough, especially if you, like me, didn't even know boundaries existed until you were a full-grown adult (or maybe until just now). However, it's worth the work, I promise.

How about an example? When I first started as a therapist a few years ago, my first permanent position—that I worked my butt off to get, by the way—was working as a mental health and addictions counsellor in Downtown Vancouver, Canada. When I got the job I called my parents to share the great news, but instead of rounds of applause and congratulations I was met with anxiety from my dad. The office was in a low SES neighbourhood and he was worried about me. I knew his reaction was because he cared, but in that moment, I wasn't interested in being met with fear. I was looking for celebration. I reassured him that I would be safe, but he continued peppering me with questions about my potential clients, my colleagues, the safety protocols in place, and on and on. I wasn't interested in answering these questions; I'd just called for a pat on the back.

In that moment, I decided to make a request: "Dad, I understand you're concerned, but I feel good about this job, and don't feel unsafe working there. Let's talk about how great it's going to be instead of going over and over all the *potential* negatives!"

When he kept asking for the details I didn't want to discuss, I set a boundary: "Dad, I've said I don't want to talk about it further. We can either talk about something else or we can talk another time." That's a boundary. *If this is what* you *need to do, this is what* I *need to do.*

Boundaries are about learning to accept that people will do what they choose to do, and giving yourself permission to do the same. Trying to force someone to change won't work; you have no control over any person besides yourself. You can ask for someone to change. In many relationships people are willing to respect at least some requests and limits. However, when they're not, you only have a couple of options. Option 1: You can reconsider your boundary due to their inability to change. Or Option 2: You can do what you need to take care of you.

For example, if the same relative makes critical comments about you every time you're together at a family gathering, even after you've asked them to stop, it's likely that they will continue to do so. If you don't like it, you can accept that those comments will keep coming and just choose not to engage on the topic, or you can remove yourself from the conversation altogether. Boundaries.

Got it? Believe me, it takes practice. However, if you're ready to take boundaries to the next level, you can also work on managing your mind. Let's say, for example, that your mother-in-law makes a comment about your weight. You can stay in the situation and decide what said comment means to you. Perhaps she is awful, rude, and mean. Or you can run it through an ABCBO and make it mean whatever you want. She may be commenting about your weight because she's anxious about her own, or she may have internalized fat-phobia, or maybe she's always been criticized about her weight, so she's passing on a family tradition. They can think what they want, and so can you.

Who makes up the rules?

Boundaries are also not about forcing others to play by your rules. They're about setting your own rules and following through on them. Boundaries say to the world, "These are my rules, and if you want to play together, that's great. If you don't want to play by my rules, that's fine. I just reserve the right to decide whether or not I'm going to continue playing."

Speaking of what boundaries are *not*—they are also not manipulation. When you were a kid, you might have said, "If you're not going to play my way, then I won't play with you at all." Not going to get you far. Boundaries sound more like, "You can do what you want. If I don't like it and I ask you to stop, but you won't, I'm not going to play." Everyone has the right to determine who they are and what they do. If you set boundaries to control or manipulate, it's not going to end well because, again, your boundaries aren't about others, they are about you.

Let's come back to the baseline mantra of healthy boundaries: *If this is what you need to do, this is what I need to do.* When my eldest daughter was a baby, my parents would come to our house to babysit every Friday while I worked. I was grateful for their generous help. The only downside was they would often arrive several minutes late. Unfortunately, this increment of time would make me late for work, and I was beginning to feel highly stressed about it every week.

I asked them if they could really try to be on time, and though I believe they made an effort, they weren't always successful. At this point, I had choices. I couldn't change them and I had made my request, so I could have said, "Thank you for everything, but this isn't working out. Let's schedule grandparent time on non-workdays." While this would have been a disappointment, it was an option.

However, I devised another option that didn't involve scrapping the whole thing. I told them I needed to leave for work at 10 a.m. sharp, so if they weren't at my house by then, I would begin to walk to work with the baby in the stroller. This way, they could meet me on the way, and we'd do an en route baby transfer.

Yes, packing up a baby required extra time and effort on already busy mornings. And, yes, having to slightly alter their route to meet us required something extra from them. But ultimately, this arrangement took the bigger pressure off everyone. This wasn't an attempt at manipulation. This was my choice based on their choice. They chose to be late, and I chose to leave on time with the baby. In the long run, once they realized how important it was to me, they started coming on time more often. However, the curbside baby shuffle worked fine the times when they just couldn't make it happen.

Just Say No?

A big part of having healthy boundaries is learning how to say no. I have a feeling you could create a long list of things in your life that you've said yes to that you wish you hadn't. There are the obvious ones, like saying yes to your boss's "quick" favor at the end of the workday for the third time this week. Or calling your mom because you know she wants you to, but then you can't get off the phone for hours even though you can see countless things piling onto your plate as she chats away. Or agreeing to attend several gatherings on the first nice weekend in a month when all you want is some quiet time to yourself.

Then there are the less obvious ones, like the after-work drink with a friend that you know will result in an extra-late night of preparation for your presentation the next day. Or volunteering when you're already overwhelmed with everything as it is. Or agreeing to make dinner for yourself and all your roommates because they're tired… but you're also tired.

Saying "no" can be hard. I get it. Instead, though, you take on and do too much to avoid it. However, have you ever wondered why "no" is so hard to say? Why do you feel bad about it? Which of your thoughts are preventing this particular two-letter word from escaping your lips?

Boundary-Blocking Thoughts

Before we delve further into boundaries, you need to recognize some underlying, maybe subconscious, beliefs you have about boundaries that prevent you from setting them. Behavior is never for no reason, so you must be getting something from living a boundary-less life. You may want to have them, but you know by now there must be something standing in your way. Yep, you got it. Your thoughts are keeping you from them.

While this could be many different things, I want to introduce you to my friend, Secondary Gain. This concept describes when you consciously want something, but your brain subconsciously likes the reward of something else better, so it keeps defaulting to the one with the better reward. Many potential conflicting thoughts exist and block you from healthy boundaries. The more you practice challenging your default barriers, the more your brain will begin to like the alternatives. Eleven common "Boundary-Blocking Thoughts" are listed below, paired with their "Boundary-Freeing Counter-Thoughts":

- **Boundary-Blocking Thought #1**: Boundaries will make people think I'm selfish.
  Boundary-Freeing Counter-Thought: It's not my job to manage other people's thoughts; it's my job to be responsible for myself.
- **Boundary-Blocking Thought #2**: Boundaries will make people think I'm a difficult person.
  Boundary-Freeing Counter-Thought: It is not difficult to respect my own limits.
- **Boundary-Blocking Thought #3**: If I set boundaries, it will hurt people I love.
  Boundary-Freeing Counter-Thought: If I don't set a boundary, bitterness and resentment will build inside me, making me more likely to lash out at some point. Although someone may initially be hurt by my boundary, it is far better to set it than cause harm later.
- **Boundary-Blocking Thought #4**: If I set a boundary, it means I'm a mean person.
  Boundary-Freeing Counter-Thought: If I set a boundary, it means I'm a clear person.
- **Boundary-Blocking Thought #5**: If I set boundaries, I will feel way too much guilt.
  Boundary-Freeing Counter-Thought: I'll only feel guilty if I convince myself that what I want, think, need, and feel doesn't matter.
- **Boundary-Blocking Thought #6**: If I set a boundary, I'll make someone uncomfortable.
  Boundary-Freeing Counter-Thought: I may. But my comfort counts, too.
- **Boundary-Blocking Thought #7**: I can't say no when someone asks something of me.
  Boundary-Freeing Counter-Thought: I have a right to say no when I want or need to.
- **Boundary-Blocking Thought #8**: It is my duty to hold the group/family together, and therefore I can't say no or take a step back.

Boundary-Freeing Counter-Thought: It is up to individuals in any community to contribute to the wellbeing of the group and their own wellbeing.

- **Boundary-Blocking Thought #9**: If I say no, people will not like or value me. I'll be alone.
  Boundary-Freeing Counter-Thought: Some people will not like to hear me say no; others will respect me more for it. I am more than what I can do for others.
- **Boundary-Blocking Thought #10**: It doesn't matter how people treat me. If I keep quiet, everyone will be happy.
  Boundary-Freeing Counter-Thought: Conflict is not forbidden. Everyone, including me, has the right to be seen, heard, and considered.
- **Boundary-Blocking Thought #11**: If I do everything for everyone, no one can criticize me, and I'll be safe.
  Boundary-Freeing Counter-Thought: It is costing me a lot to over-function; compassionate honesty is better than resentment.

Be clear, concise, and nice: How to say no

By now you're starting to chip away at your own boundary resistance. Getting into the right mindset and giving yourself the freedom to say no without fearing indefinite exile is essential. When you're new to boundary-setting, the mechanics of how to set a "no" boundary while still being respectful can be difficult to wrap your head around. The last thing I want is for boundary-setting to be an alienating experience.

When you're setting a boundary, it's important to be clear, not wishy-washy or tentative. Don't pull out a "Maybe" or an "I'm not sure" when you really mean "No." Being clear allows both parties to move on without trying to find a good excuse to back out (you) or being left hoping and waiting (them). And although it might feel awkward at first, clarity is a sign of respect. You're not leaving anyone hanging out to dry and you're honoring yourself in your wish to decline.

Also, be concise. People have the tendency to over-explain and present reasons for their "no." Giving a 10-minute soliloquy about how your kids, the dog, and your partner have all banded together to prevent you from committing just isn't necessary. Most people just want an answer. It's fine to give a reason if you want to, but there's no need to over-justify or over-apologize. "I have another commitment" is a perfectly reasonable explanation, even if your other commitment is a night all to yourself watching *Friends* reruns. If what you need is some Ross and Rachel in your life, that's what you need. No monologue of apology necessary.

Finally, be nice. This goes a long way. People are usually fine with "no" if you're nice about it. Start with some version of "thank you" if it fits. *Thank you for thinking of me, thank you for offering me the opportunity, it was nice of you to consider me.* And then get to the clear and concise part. You'll be surprised how easily people accept "no" when you're nice about it.

EXERCISE: 25 WAYS TO SAY "NO"

Finding the right words to say "no" can be tricky, especially if you're new to it and find it anxiety-provoking and uncomfortable. I've compiled a list of 25 ways to say "no" that fit the bill for clear, concise, and nice. Free up space for what you want by practicing the effective "no":

1. Thanks for asking, but unfortunately my schedule is full.
2. Thanks for the offer, but I have another commitment at that time.
3. Thanks for the invitation, but my schedule is packed to the brim right now! Please keep me in mind for something like this in the future. (Only say this if you mean it.)
4. I would love to say yes, but unfortunately, I need to say no.
5. No, but thanks for reaching out.

---

6. Unfortunately, I'm unable to help you with this. All the best.
7. Thanks for thinking of me. But right now, I'm not able to.
8. I'm not interested, thank you anyway.
9. Thanks for asking, but unfortunately, I'll have to decline.
10. Unfortunately, now is not a good time for me.
11. Thanks for the offer, but I am having a hard time keeping up with the commitments I already have, so I have to say no.
12. Sorry, I'm not able to do that.
13. I am fully committed at this time, but thanks for thinking of me.
14. I wish I could say yes, but I need to say no.
15. No, that doesn't work for me unfortunately.
16. Sorry, I can't.
17. My schedule is booked, but thanks anyway.
18. I don't think I'm the best fit for this. Thanks for thinking of me, though.
19. I'm sorry, but I'm not able to do this right now.
20. I have already outlined my priorities for this month and am unable to commit to anything else.
21. Sorry, I can't take that on.
22. I'm unable to help currently. All the best on your search.
23. I'd love to, but I have another commitment.
24. I am at my limit for extra commitments right now—thanks for the offer.
25. No, thank you. (Isn't this one such a chic, timeless classic?)

I used to feel obligated to say yes to everything and everyone that came my way. I didn't want to seem ungrateful or rude. The problem with this was I was saying too many false yesses, after which I would be in a state of dread. I wasn't sure how I'd make it through everything I had committed to on any given day.

On top of it, I was also bitter and resentful toward the people who kept asking me to do things. But why would they stop if I continued to say yes?

So instead of keeping this cycle going, I decided to add "no" to my vocabulary. Do you know what happened? Not a whole lot. Some people were a little confused by my sudden discovery of that little two-letter word, but the world didn't come to an end. I didn't lose business, friends, or family. My marriage was fine. No one abandoned me. Wait, that's not totally true. Something did happen. I felt happier, lighter, and more free.

Boundaries will set you free

It may sound counterintuitive, but healthy boundaries will set you free. When you start taking charge of your life and choices, you will have the freedom to navigate life the way you want to. Being in the driver's seat of your own life also means you aren't stopping everything to wait for others to change. We touched on this earlier when we talked about fusing our emotional state with someone else's. This fusion is called codependence and it's exactly what it sounds like: our mental and emotional state is dependent on another person's. If you are living in a state of codependence, learning to have, set, and keep your healthy boundaries is key to unraveling that emotional entanglement.

It's important to note that having boundaries will not make you devoid of empathy. Compassionate, empathic people can be amazing boundary-setters and still care about their fellow humans' experiences. When you fully believe that what you want, think, need, and feel counts as much as what everyone else does, you'll also take responsibility for your mental and emotional state. You can empathize and sympathize with others' feelings without taking responsibility for them. If we're honest, the responsibility for others' thoughts and feelings was never yours in the first place.

EXERCISE: THE CIRCLE OF RESPONSIBILITY

You are responsible for you. You are not responsible for any other independent adult. You know why? You can't be responsible for something or someone you have no control over. Therefore, because you have no control over anyone else's thoughts, feelings, beliefs, ideas, ideals, choices, or life, you can't be responsible for them. Do you know who you *are* responsible for? Yourself (and your dependents if you have them). The reasoning is the same. You are in charge of your thoughts, feelings, choices, and life. Therefore, you are responsible for them. So, you are responsible for yourself and you are not responsible for others.

Of note: this is not a green light to run around being a jerk to everyone else because, "Hey, Julia said I'm not responsible *for* anyone." When it comes to other humans, you do have responsibility. You are responsible *to* them. You are responsible to be kind, respectful, caring, and at least half decent. You're not responsible *for* them though. The *for* only applies to you.

The Circle of Responsibility (opposite) outlines examples of what you are and are not responsible for in your daily life. As you go through the next day or two, take note of which things you habitually take responsibility for outside of your circle. And when you look over your notes, ask yourself how you feel when you attempt to control the uncontrollable and what it would be like if you stopped. I reference this visual whenever I find myself crossing the line of my own responsibility, and I invite you to do the same.

The Circle of Responsibility

TAKEAWAYS

- Boundaries are not about changing anyone else; they are about taking responsibility for yourself.
- We struggle to set boundaries or say no because we have boundary-blocking thoughts that prevent us from doing so.
- When setting a boundary, be nice, clear, and concise.
- You are responsible *to* others, but you are only responsible *for* yourself.

Journal prompt: What would be different in my life if I gave myself the freedom and permission to set boundaries whenever I wanted or needed to?

CHAPTER 19
STOP PEOPLE-PLEASING

People-pleasing, much like perfectionism, is often worn like a badge of honor. On the surface, we claim it as a flaw, but it doesn't sound that bad when you say it out loud. In fact, it almost sounds… good. "Oh my, I'm such people-pleaser," they say coyly, while the subtext says, "I'm such a super-nice person who goes above and beyond for others, even to my own detriment." On the contrary, these saint-like characteristics are not wonderful and admirable like you may be tempted to think. In essence, people-pleasing is people-misleading.

When you're constantly doing what other people want and being who other people want for their approval, you're covertly misleading them about who you really are. No one loves pleasing at their own expense 100 per cent of the time. Editing out the real you so people see you inauthentically is essentially lying. Do you genuinely want to pretend and perform for everyone else for the rest of your life? Eesh. I hope not.

In defense of all the people-pleasers out there, including you if you are one, the pleasing trap happens because of the desire to build relationships and feel connected to others. But the hard truth is, even if you do win approval, it won't feel as wonderful as you thought because the approval and connection aren't based on authenticity. If people feel connected to you because you please them, you've created a connection based on a false version of yourself, so it won't feel real. If we dig deeper into the minds of people-pleasers, much of their behavior is rooted in a sense of unworthiness. Their underlying belief about themselves often sounds something like, "If I can be who others want me to be, then they'll like me, and if they like me and think I'm a good person, then maybe I'll believe it, too."

Don't get me wrong, people-pleasing is not the same as being kind, caring, generous, and compassionate. I'm for any and all of those attributes. They are different because in their truest sense, kindness, care, generosity, and compassion are expressions of the beautiful parts of ourselves, not crafted personas created to get approval. One of these comes with pure intentions and makes you feel lovely, light, and easy. The other is riddled with draining resentment and stress. I'm willing to bet you know which is which.

People-pleasing is also saying nothing

As much as people-pleasing is defined by the things we do and say to control how others feel about us, it's equally defined by the things we don't do or say. Have you ever avoided speaking up because you didn't want to rock the boat or disturb the peace? Have you missed opportunities to speak up about racist, sexist, or inappropriate comments because you didn't want to make anyone feel uncomfortable? This type of silence is also people-pleasing.

Here's the tough part, friend. To break the cycle of people-pleasing deceit, you need to take a step back and really ask yourself if you're willing to live with a decrease in your admiration points in exchange for an increase in your authenticity points. Ask yourself: *Am I willing to be honest about who I am, how much I'm willing to do, what I like and don't like, and what's okay and not okay with me, what I believe to be right and wrong, at the cost of changing people's opinions and maybe even losing certain people?*

If you decide you're willing to accept the consequences that might come with speaking up, standing up, setting limits, doing less, and being honest about who you truly are, not who you want others to think you are, then let's go ahead and do this thing! Because you are absolutely correct—everyone else's comfort and happiness doesn't need to be put before your own all the time. You count. Remember?

I think it's time we ask the big question. Why did you ever think you didn't count anyways? Why did you think your wants, needs, and feelings don't matter? We're about to go back into your formative years. Did you grow up in a home where love was dependent on you being exactly who your parents thought you should be? Did you have to perform, perfect, please, produce, or placate to earn love and approval? Did you learn early on that other people's wants and needs mattered more than yours?

Let's hop to the now. Do you still believe your lovability is correlated to meeting (or anticipating) other people's wants, needs, and preferences to make them happy? Do you think you have an equal place in your relationships, or do you find yourself hustling for your worthiness? Maybe this isn't totally conscious and you didn't even realize you've been doing this until now. Regardless, it's worth taking a few minutes to think about. Where did that people-pleasing come from?

It's an inside job

We people-please for outside approval because if *they* do, then we hope *we* will, too. If you want to stop outsourcing how you feel about yourself to others, it's time to do the inner work and get clear on how you feel about yourself. To be real, it's pretty hard to feel good about someone who's constantly neglecting your wants, needs, boundaries, and preferences. And if you're being that person to you—which is exactly what you're doing when you people-please—how can you feel good about yourself?

You have to be good to yourself first. The better you treat yourself by listening to and respecting your feelings, recognizing your strengths, and choosing to think encouraging and supportive thoughts, the better you'll feel. If you don't self-abandon, you won't be compelled to people-please to prevent abandonment from others. You'll know what relationships are supposed to feel like.

Know your priorities

When you know yourself and feel secure in what is most important to you, the temptation to people-please all but disappears. It's easy to let a request from someone else take priority when you neglect what matters to you. The more you say yes to someone else's priorities, the less you say yes to your own. Not to say you should never be willing to step up and help someone else, but what's most important to you is as worthy of your time, attention, and intention as whatever the person is asking.

An easy way to keep yourself focused on what matters to you is to first decide what those things are. Sounds simple, right? But here's where we frequently get tripped up. Sometimes, in our attempt to focus on what's important to us, we get overexcited and end up picking way too many priorities. "I want to advance my career, teach my two-year-old to read, learn to crochet, read a new book each week, go to the gym every other day, spend more time with my aging parents, start the side business, meditate for an hour every morning, renovate the bathroom, volunteer at the local food bank, and learn to make puff pastry from scratch." And this, dear human, is the recipe for burnout.

Instead, here's your task. You are going to pick five things. Five. Identify which five things are your top priorities. These are the things you are going to spend about 90 per cent of your time on in your life. I know it can be hard to narrow down. Here are some ideas: time with your children (nieces and nephews count), time with your partner, time with your parents, building your business, working toward a promotion, time with friends, working out regularly, cooking from scratch, spending time religiously or spiritually engaged, writing a book, reading books, etc. You get the idea. Before you get going, note your five priorities will change depending on the season of life you're occupying at a given moment in time.

If you're wondering, my five are:

1. Spending quality time with my kids
2. Spending quality time with my husband
3. Building my business
4. Exercising daily
5. Being with my extended family (especially my parents as they live close by).

And that's it. This makes it really easy for me to prioritize when a request comes my way. All I have to do is ask myself if it falls into one of my top five priorities. If not, it's an easy no. And if it does, I take some time to consider it and go from there.

You might notice that "spending time with friends" isn't on my list. I learned the hard way that if I try to add anything else to my list of priorities, I'll burn out. That said, I do come up with little hacks to see my friends semi-regularly, by combining friend time with another priority that is on my list. For example, play dates at the park with one of my best friends and her kids so that while the kids play, we moms can, too. Another way I get friend time is combining it with husband time by going out on a double date. But if a friend calls and asks to go get a coffee? Most of the time, my answer is no, but I may counter-offer getting together for a power walk. See what I did there?

EXERCISE: DEFINE YOUR TOP FIVE PRIORITIES

You don't get a medal for racing from one thing to the next, being and doing everything for everyone from dawn until dusk. What you get from that is copious anxiety and exhaustion with a side of resentment. So, it's time. It's time to sit down and decide on your top five priorities in your life right now. What are they? Your health? Your immediate family? Your extended

---

family? Your friends? Your job? Your spiritual or religious community? Your business? Your schoolwork? A favorite hobby or passion project? Renovating your house?

It may be hard to narrow your priorities down at first, but it's even harder to keep up with more than five, isn't it? Remember, these are the five items you are going to dedicate 90 per cent of your time to on most days. And anything that doesn't fall into one of your priorities will either be a hard no or combined with one of your top five (if you want).

Once you have your list, use it as a guide for planning your life. Don't forget that everything that you say no to gives you a yes slot in return. When you effectively prioritize, you'll create enough space for what matters most to you.

TAKEAWAYS

- People-pleasing is people-misleading. It prevents you from connecting honestly and authentically with others.
- The key to moving past people-pleasing starts with bolstering your self-worth from the inside.
- Use prioritization as a method to identify what is important to your core self. Begin to tease out which requests are about your own needs, and which are about those of others.

Journal prompt: When and with whom do I notice myself engaging in people-pleasing? What am I afraid will happen if I stop?

CHAPTER 20
MESSING WITH THE SYSTEM

Before we talk about buckling into the driver's seat and taking charge of all our unhelpful behaviors, we need to address something. Setting boundaries, no longer rearranging your life for others, and spending more time on what is important to you is a change. This part of your journey is obvious. What may not be quite as obvious is that there will be people in your life who will not be a fan of these changes. Not everyone will protest, of course, but some will—and with gusto.

We human beings and our brains find change difficult, as you know. Side note: I do find this ironic considering we're also an incredibly adaptable species. Anyways, although we find making changes in our own lives difficult, we find it even harder when other people make changes in ways that affect us.

When you change how you show up in your relationships or revamp your priorities and this alters what you're offering and available for, you're changing someone else's life. They've come to expect certain things from you. You've been a certain way with them, so they assume you are going to continue with the same. And now that you're not, some people may not like it, especially those who have benefited from your self-neglect. This is not because they are bad people. Chances are, they had no idea their expectations haven't been completely reasonable. Why would they if, up until now, you've been meeting every single one?

The effect of your changes will probably be the most apparent in your closest, longest relationships. This, for many of us, is with our family. And also like many of us, our relationship with family is functionally dysfunctional at best. I tend to compare family dynamics to an old factory with turning widgets and cogs. The widgets and cogs work in a technical sense and have for a long time. Sure, they've been spitting out product that's coming down the conveyor belt just a little wrong for years, but the output is acceptable and functional enough for everyone to accept that this is just the way our factory performs. Sure, the products are more fragile than intended and, yes, the glue isn't holding quite as well as you'd like, but, you know, nothing is perfect!

But now you, an integral cog in the dysfunctional machine, have wriggled out of place, and the whole factory is an utter disaster. So, what does the factory do? Well, it wants you to reconsider immediately, dysfunction aside, so it sets off all kinds of alarms attempting to coerce you into staying the way you were. Your family, your partner, or even your close friends may try to convince you the factory of dysfunction is in fine working order by whatever means necessary and will crumble if you change. But you know better now, don't you?

They may accuse you and your new boundaries of being selfish. They may use guilt trips, silent treatment, or manipulative statements like, "I would never do something like that to you," and, "What do you think you're doing? That's not how we do things in this family," or even, "I thought you loved me." They may openly criticize you or say you're being ridiculous or difficult. They might make passive-aggressive comments such as, "Well, I guess that's Julia setting one of her boundaries again!" (I may be speaking from experience here.) Underneath all of this behavior, though, is probably confusion, hurt, and a little fear, because it feels like you're pulling away. They may even think you don't care about them anymore.

None of their reactions mean you should stop. Just like you, they decide how they see things, think about things, and feel about things. And just like you, they can start down a new path any time.

Your response

After the drama, you're probably wondering how to encourage those around you to be on board with the more self-differentiated you. How do you help them to accept you as an individual with your own limits, boundaries, and a stronger sense of who you are? First, be patient.

Second, make sure they know your changes are not *against* them. You are making changes *for* you. There's a big difference. You're not making different choices to punish them; you're altering your choices to preserve yourself. Some will understand and respect this fairly quickly, while others will need time to adjust. And, sure, a few may stop returning your calls because perhaps they really only valued you for your "yes," or they can't cope with their own anxiety related to the shift in the relationship dynamics.

Pushback related to your personal journey to change will feel hard and may tempt you to throw in the towel because going back to the way things were is easier. But it wasn't easier, remember? The difficulty of being self-neglecting and boundary-less is why you started making the changes in the first place. When you face resistance, choose thoughts that will help keep you focused, moving forward, and fulfilling your deep desire to feel more calm, confident, and in charge of your life and choices. Remind yourself that you are your own person with your own wants, needs, preferences, and limits; and you have the responsibility to respect and communicate them as a mature and emotionally grounded adult.

Tantrums

When you are dealing with resistance, it's helpful to mentally compare the resisters to toddlers. I'm not saying they are babies, but adults often oppose change similarly to small children, usually with fewer tantrums, but not always. In this scenario, imagine whoever is pushing back on your personal changes as a child you're taking to the grocery store. Up until now, every time you have them waiting in the checkout line, you've bought them candy while you wait. Then one day you realize the child now expects candy every single time you're in line. Because you don't want the child to become dependent on treats—that won't be a great long-term trait—you decide to stop with the checkout line treats.

You know what's going to happen the first time you say no to the checkout line treat, right? The child's going to freak out. They're going to yell, scream, cry, and may even proclaim they hate you. And this likely isn't the only time this will happen. No, they're going to throw a fit the next few times you're in line if you keep setting the boundary and saying no. But eventually, they will understand you're not messing around, and you are not buying them candy, so they will stop asking—or at the very least they'll stop losing their ever-living mind when you turn them down.

Your job is to stick to your boundary and not give in. You wouldn't give in to the tantrums of a toddler in response to a limit, so don't go back on asking your mother-in-law to call first before she "stops by." If you cave, it sends the message that your boundaries are negotiable and you don't really mean them, so they don't have to be taken seriously. If you want your boundaries to be respected, you need to respect them, too.

I'm not going to promise an absolute 100 per cent success rate, but most people eventually come to accept the changes others make in their lives, even when they may not be too excited about them at first. Although brains may protest, people are capable of respecting who you are and what you're able to offer, and they'll adjust their expectations accordingly. The good news is, after you weather the resistance storm, your relationships will be stronger and healthier, and so will you.

I remember when I first started setting boundaries. I was the recipient of underhanded remarks and some not-so-subtle judgment; I caught wind of my family talking about me and my "fancy new boundaries" behind my back. But I didn't give up. I knew my life deserved this from me. And guess what? They eventually came around and their expectations of me changed because I was more authentic, clear, and direct in my communication.

And do you know what the best part was? Many of my original resisters started to realize the whole boundary thing was not the terrible idea they once thought it was and, one at a time, they started setting their own healthier boundaries for themselves. That's the thing about this work. When you see how much happier people become as they're doing it, you can't help but want some of it, too. Healthy boundaries are contagious, and I am here for all of it.

EXERCISE: THOUGHTS TO STAY THE COURSE

My friend, I can't emphasize enough the importance of you sticking to setting healthy boundaries for yourself, even if you are met with opposition from those you hold dear. To prepare yourself for this potential, take a moment and write down five thoughts you can have that will remind you to stay the course. Here are a few examples to get you started:

- Healthy boundaries will set me free.
- My wants, needs, and preferences count too, and it's up to me to communicate them.
- If I can respect others' boundaries, they can respect mine.

- Setting boundaries may feel hard now, but the more I practice, the easier setting them will be.
- Saying no isn't a crime, even if it upsets someone.
- There is more to me than just my "yes."

Keep showing up with your healthy boundaries. I believe in you and you should, too.

Other people's boundaries

If you want others to respect your boundaries, this same courtesy must be extended to others. You may think this is obvious and assume that when you start basking in the glorious exhale of better boundary-setting, you'll automatically be fine on the receiving end of other people's boundaries. But I can tell you from personal experience that's not always the case.

I was so pleased with myself for finding my guilt-free, boundary-setting voice with my family. Then, one day, my older sister found hers and I jumped right into the role of resister. I liked the freedom of setting whatever boundary I wanted, but when she began to offer herself the same freedom, I was not on board. I'd been getting used to speaking up for what I did and didn't want but didn't realize that, as a result, my sister had been losing herself by just going along with me.

One day, when my resistance was in full force (although I didn't realize it), my sister said to me—clearly, concisely, and nicely—"Hey, if you can have boundaries then I can, too." In that moment I realized that, yes, as uncomfortable as I was at first, this was fair and true. It takes a level of emotional maturity to allow yourself to say no, but supporting someone else's right to do so is a whole new skill set you might just learn along the way.

If you ever find yourself put off by someone else's boundaries, take that moment of sacred pause and examine your thoughts. Are you thinking they're being difficult, unreasonable, or selfish?

If the roles were reversed, would this still be true? Or could it simply be that they are looking out for themselves? If you are going to expect boundary-understanding from others, expect no less from yourself.

TAKEAWAYS

- Resistance to your boundaries doesn't indicate you're doing anything wrong.
- It's important to stay consistent with your boundaries. Most people will come around eventually.
- If you're going to set boundaries, make sure you're okay when others set theirs.

Journal prompt: Who am I worried about upsetting with my boundaries? What will I say to myself if this happens?

CHAPTER 21

DEAL WITH DIFFICULT PEOPLE AND HAVE BETTER RELATIONSHIPS

Want something to chew on for a few minutes?

Most people in difficult relationships don't think they're the difficult one. Most believe it's the other person who's being selfish, difficult, disrespectful, controlling, or demanding. But how can that be? How can two people in the same relationship believe they are right and the other person is wrong? I can tell you. Every human on the planet is walking around with their own ideas about how people should and should not be. Every single one of us has our very own rulebook.

The rulebook

Whether conscious or not, we all have strong ideas about how things *should* be, how others *should* be, how life *should* be, and how the world *should* be. We have thoughts about what makes a good person, what it means to demonstrate respect for others, and how soon someone should reciprocate a favor. We even have rules about reasonable levels of household cleanliness and how long is too long to wait for a text message reply. We also operate as if our personal rules are not mere ideas, but obvious expectations based on facts everyone knows. Therefore when someone doesn't comply, they are breaking the rules. In reality, though, they are not breaking *the* rules; they are breaking *our* rules.

And this is where the trouble starts. We assume everyone has the same rulebook and judge them based on our copy. We interact with one another as if everyone sees the world the same way we do. But everyone has their own rulebook, many of which are wildly different from our own. Even those closest to us may have vastly different rules for how they govern their own lives and how others should govern theirs.

When some of our rules overlap with other rulebooks, we feel like we must be right. But some will not overlap at all, which brings us back to square one, where there is no one set of rules for us to follow. If you find yourself questioning the audacity of someone in a given situation, it's less likely they are actually a horrible person, and more likely they are, in fact, just following their rules and not yours.

Your overbearing parent doesn't think they're being overbearing; they think they're trying to prevent you from making a mistake. Your unsolicited-advice-giving mother-in-law doesn't think she's overstepping; she thinks she's giving you fantastic parenting tips from her years of experience. Your hard-headed siblings don't think they're criticizing your choices; they think they know what's best and are trying to force— *ahem* I mean *graciously share* their knowledge with you. Your only-points-out-your-mistakes boss doesn't think they're being demoralizing; they think they're giving you constructive notes and you don't need to be coddled with a positive feedback sandwich. And your nosey coworker doesn't think she's prying; she thinks it's perfectly reasonable to know what's what about everyone in the office. They are all playing by their own rules, and so are you.

Now, you don't have to agree with or even like their rules, but this is why empathy is important. If you're able to understand that while they are breaking your rules, they are fully adhering to their own, it may keep you from being quite so offended or upset, especially when you're applying all your other tools.

Why are people difficult?

Most people aren't intentionally being difficult. In fact, they don't think they're being difficult at all. They believe they're typical, rational, and reasonable people because they are acting in accordance with what their rulebook defines as typical, rational, and reasonable behavior. Here's the even harder truth: we find people difficult not because of what they're doing, but because (surprise!) of our thoughts about what they're doing. To us it's obviously not right, but to them, it's probably just fine.

For example, your partner might have a completely different definition of the word "messy" in their rulebook. If they routinely leave their dirty socks in the middle of the carpet, or leave dishes in the sink overnight, you might think they're being lazy or disrespectful. In their brain, where their rulebook lives, socks on the floor and dishes in the sink do not compute as problems. According to their rules, they'll get to the socks and the mound of dishes at some point, which is acceptable. However, perhaps according to your rules, homes should be spick-and-span before your head hits the pillow each night.

And doesn't this lead to quite the conundrum. To you, they're being lazy and irresponsible. To them, you're being rigid and uptight. In these moments we may forget that rarely are people doing things against us; they are usually doing things for themselves in accordance with what makes sense in their heads. There is a big difference between the two.

EXERCISE: MY RULES/YOUR RULES

I want you to think about five rules in your rulebook that are different from those of a loved one—this can be your partner, a parent, a sibling, an adult child, or a close friend. You might find this most helpful if you consider a person with whom you have relationship struggles. Once you've considered the rules that differ between your rulebooks, ask yourself what would change if you were able to see these differences not as mean, terrible, or wrong, but simply as them acting in accordance with their own rules instead of yours?

This may go without saying, but I am going to say it just in case. This concept does not promote excusing or tolerating abusive or harmful behavior. This concept is best applied in situations when we believe someone is acting in a way we find difficult based on our thoughts. Harmful behavior and abuse, whether it's acceptable in someone's rulebook or not, is not an excusable misunderstanding or perspective-taking issue.

I don't get their rules

Sometimes we'll be able to understand someone's rules and be okay playing by them. My husband lets the dishes pile up beside the sink so he can efficiently wash several at a time. Even though it irritates me because I hate dirty dishes sitting on the counter, I understand the lack of efficiency that comes with washing a single fork at a time. I do understand his rule and live with it, even if I don't like it.

And then there are some rules we'll never fully comprehend.

A few years ago, I made a deep, fast friend. You know the type of friend you meet for the first time and feel like you've known a lifetime? That was us. We met at a professional workshop and from the moment we introduced ourselves we couldn't stop talking. We spent most of the workshop together and after returning to our respective homes, we continued to build our friendship. I loved her. We had a deep understanding and a beautiful appreciation for one another. It was as if we understood each other in that I-can't-quite-explain-it-but-it-feels-different-than-my-other-friends kind of way.

One day we were out for coffee, just over a year after we'd met. We were having a great conversation about learning to believe in ourselves when suddenly (at least to me), she asked me how much time I spent working on my "money mindset." I was perplexed. This question seemed to have come out of nowhere. After a moment of racking my brain for any past money mindset seminars I'd attended (which, to date, had been zero), I admitted that, as a business owner, I hadn't spent much time working on my money mindset. She replied in a half-accusatory, half-angry tone that I was being an irresponsible and selfish businesswoman by not focusing on this area.

I didn't understand what was happening. How had our conversation gone from learning to trust who we are to the inevitability of my business going up in flames because I hadn't been reciting my abundance mantras?

The conversation eventually died down because, honestly, I didn't really even know what a money mindset was at the time. Then we went our separate ways. And that was the last time I saw this friend I'd grown so close to in such a short amount of time. We did have two or three abrupt and uncomfortable telephone conversations after that day, but nothing since then.

I spent a lot of time wondering what I had done wrong that had upset her so greatly. For a while, I took it personally and thought I'd caused her to treat me that way. But I hadn't. Somewhere in her rulebook it probably said something like, "If someone does something you find irresponsible (or whatever she may say to describe what happened), it's okay to criticize them and end the relationship."

Whether or not I like or agree with her rule, it's hers. Yes, I could have reached out to her to find out why she'd gotten so angry with me about something I thought so trivial, but I decided not to. Because according to my rulebook, angry outbursts with no explanation or attempt at reconciliation are unkind and disrespectful. And that's not the kind of friendship I want to foster.

Understanding you have your rules and others have theirs is helpful, especially if you're trying to take things less personally. It reinforces the idea that people aren't against us, but for themselves. My husband wasn't leaving the dishes on the counter to be difficult, lazy, or contrary to my cleanliness rules—even if he was, it still wouldn't have been about me—he was following his rule that says, "Wait to do the dishes until there are enough dishes to be worth washing." And my former friend wasn't criticizing me because I'd done something objectively wrong. It was something to do with whatever is in her rulebook. I'll never know.

We can't make people play by our rules, just like other people cannot force us to play by theirs. We can make a request for rule amendments, such as, "If my office door is closed, please come in only if it's urgent," or, "Please do not yell or call me names during an argument. It's not okay with me." The other party may or may not comply. And if your request is declined, you get to decide whether you can accept their unwillingness to play by your rule, negotiate until you find a middle ground, or set a boundary.

TAKEAWAYS

- Every human has their own set of rules regarding what behaviors, choices, or ways of existing in the world are reasonable and acceptable.
- We judge people as "difficult" when they are often just behaving in a way that is not in line with our own beliefs and desires (i.e., our rulebook).
- Other people's rulebooks help us to understand that other people are acting "for" themselves, not "against" us.

Journal prompt: Which rules of a loved one can I work on accepting even if I don't like them?

CHAPTER 22
STOP OVERTHINKING

What if I mess up in the meeting tomorrow? What if I don't wake up when my alarm goes off in the morning? What if I don't have enough time to finish the assignment? What if I get fired? What if my partner leaves me? Why hasn't my friend texted me back yet? Is she mad at me? What if my team loses? What if I forget to drop off those forms? Why did I do that? What did they mean by that? Why the heck did I say that? What are they thinking about me now? Why did I have to go through that?

Overthinking about tomorrow, overthinking about yesterday, stressing about stressing, spinning about sinning, and worrying about every glimmer of a possibility sure does put a damper on life, huh? We obsess about the maybes, the mights, and the could-bes. We replay past mess-ups on a loop in our minds. And here's the real question: Why? Why do we lease so much of our brain's real estate to what hasn't happened, likely won't, or already has?

Ground control

We've talked extensively about the human brain's borderline obsession with control, and we know it's not for no reason. Your brain thinks the more control it has, the less vulnerable it will be. It's a good thought, especially since the main job of your brain is to keep you alive as long as possible. The more control it has, the more alive you stay. Sounds reasonable.

The problem is really our go-to strategy of overthinking every possible (read: terrible) outcome when these outcomes are not actual threats to our existence. Overstressing about your 10-minute presentation scheduled for Thursday when it's only Monday morning, which impacts your ability to focus all week, is not an efficient use of our time. Whether you kill it, give a passable performance, or screw up, it's not a matter of life and death. Sure, you want to do well. If you spend a reasonable amount of time preparing, you probably will. And even if it sucks, you can chalk it up to a lesson for next time.

For many, the swirling stressful thoughts keeping you awake at night are not about whether or not you'll have enough food to eat or fresh water to drink—although I do recognize for some these concerns are very real. However, I'm guessing for the majority of those who purchased or borrowed this book, the thoughts keeping you up are about something that didn't go exactly how you wanted it to, the fear of something inane you'll have forgotten by next week, or about what someone inconsequential thinks of you. While some of these circumstances might lead to some inconveniences, discomforts, or difficult decisions, they're not true threats. If this sounds like you, let's get to the part about digging deep and doing something about these worry-filled thoughts.

There's a difference between planned and prepared versus paranoid and perfectionistic. Stop and think about it. Do you know what you're really stressed and worried about? We often experience generic feelings of dread about what might happen if things in general don't go to plan, and it isn't about anything specific at all. What is your actual fear based on? When your brain gets hijacked by worry, take a few moments to look more closely at what you're really worried about so you can decide whether it's worth the level of energy you're giving it.

The human brain loves—and I mean LOVES—a fearmongering *What if?* scenario. *What if* x *happens? What if they think* x*? What if* x *doesn't happen? What if I blow* x*? What if I have nothing to show for* x*?* And here's my wonderment. When's the last time you answered the dreaded *What if?*

I mean, what if *x* does happen? What if it doesn't? What if they think *x*? What if *x* turns out like *y*? Answer the question. What will you do? How will you handle it? How will you get through it? That pesky little question loses power fast when you answer it and play it out to the end. You may not always love the answer, but if you lay it all out there and then think about how you'll deal with the result of your *What if* scenario, it's not quite so scary.

What if I give the presentation and it falls flat? Well, you'd probably take a step back, look at the format, reflect on why it didn't land, do more research, gather more information, and put together something more compelling, because now you know what isn't.

What if I go to the party and feel awkward and uncomfortable and have no one to talk to when I get there? I don't know. You could make your way over to the food, fill your plate with hors d'oeuvres, and then casually scan the room for another awkward soul waiting to be rescued from their not-sure-what-to-do-with-themselves status.

Think about your own life. What do you notice yourself overthinking about the most? Work? Success? Money? Family dynamics? Your relationship? Friendships? Something else? Whatever it is, take a closer look at your "What if" questions and answer them. Get curious about what potential outcome you're afraid of, and then plan on how you'll deal with it if that happens. What will you do? What might you learn? How will you get through it?

Overthinking the past

Beyond the "What if" worries, we also expend copious energy dwelling on the past. We dwell on what did or didn't happen, worry about what we said or didn't say, and stress about the way things should or could have been. Have you ever asked yourself why? Or questioned the reason your brain replays things it can do nothing to change? Sure, we can learn from the past by using experiences to inform us about what does and doesn't work. But should that really require a large expanse of emotional energy? I'm going to say probably not.

If you are a reflective person, which I'm going to guess you are if you decided to read this book, you likely know what you should have done differently within the first or second replay of whatever event it is your brain won't let go. You don't need to torture yourself with 500 more replays. You've got it, you know what to do differently, and you don't really need it to plague you any longer.

So, whether you've been struggling to release something that happened last weekend or 20 years ago, here are three questions you may want to ask yourself. They may just give you a little more insight, a little more healing, and, hopefully, a little more relief:

1. *"What am I making this mean about me now?"*
   We often get caught up in our choices and experiences for years, which begs us to ask a deeper-level question: What does this mean about me now? So, ask yourself: "What am I making *x* mean about me *now*?" Once you've answered, ask this question, "Is what I'm making it mean helpful or true?" And then get right in there with your thoughts and ask yourself if you want to keep thinking them. If not, work on bringing in and believing different ones. We get to choose what we think about ourselves at each and every given moment. You can use your past to punish yourself and keep you stuck, or you can decide what you want to think today, regardless of what happened yesterday (or many yesterdays ago). This isn't about only letting your brain think about rainbows, sunshine, and unicorns. This isn't about a strict adherence to only positive thinking; this is about responsible thinking.

2. *"Do I need to be overstressing or worrying about this thing?"*
   Question: If there's something you can do about it, why worry?

   Second question: If there's nothing you can do about it, why worry?

   Worry is often a habit our brain has internalized after years of, well, worrying. Pause and take a moment to tune into your conscious mind and ask yourself if x is something you really need to be worrying about. If your brain replies with a resounding "Yes," see question 3.

3. *"Will worrying about this help?"*
   You have better ways to spend your time than stressing about what you cannot change in the past and what may (probably will not) happen in the future. If whatever you are worried about does happen in the future, remember you have the wit and the resources to handle it. You've got a life to live and love to give—and don't tell me "overthinking" was on your top five list of priorities.

EXERCISE: GETTING OUT OF YOUR HEAD

When your brain is full and emotions are running high, doing something physical can be instrumental in releasing tension. Read through the list below and choose three strategies you plan to try the next time you need to get out of your head, into your body, and find relief.

20 healthy ways to get out of your head and into your body

1. Listen to uplifting music
2. Go for a walk
3. Take a bath
4. Practice deep breathing

5. Meditate
6. Stretch
7. Dance
8. Sing or play an instrument
9. Hug someone you love
10. Create art
11. Get out and move your body
12. Have a YouTube video dance party in your living room
13. Breathe in some calming essential oils
14. Go to a park
15. Spend time with a pet
16. Complete a guided relaxation exercise
17. Garden
18. Spend time in nature
19. Play a sport
20. Get a massage

Decision freeze

Overthinking tends to wedge its way into decision-making as well. What a jerk. I'm talking decisions as trivial as, "What should I have for supper?" and as monumental as, "Is now the right time to make a career switch?" There aren't always clear or correct answers to every decision or dilemma we face, but whatever decision you make, you'll either get the outcome that you want or you'll have the opportunity to figure something out.

Realistically, you often won't know which it'll be until after you make the decision. If you get the outcome that you want, you'll look back and be glad you made the "right" decision. If your outcome doesn't go how you wanted it to, then you may regret your choice, but you'll still have something to learn from it. There's no need to blame yourself for something you could never have guaranteed. The future is never certain, nor is it fully in our control. You will drive yourself crazy if you wait for control because it will never happen. Also, you can just pick something for supper. The chances of that being a major regret are relatively low.

In fact, most of the decisions we're faced with are not a matter of life and death, and even the "wrong" decision isn't usually all that detrimental. We get stuck in the cycle of indecision because we're worried about messing up even though, in most cases, messing up doesn't matter. Like, at all. If you trust that no matter what happens, you'll figure it out, you'll unlock the antidote to fear.

Remember the "What if" exercise? Do it again, but with decisions. If you let yourself make choices instead of stalling out, you'll learn so much more from the decisions you don't get right than the ones you do. As backward as our brains seem, we humans are resilient creatures. When we get knocked down, we get back up and figure out how to move forward.

I used to be terrified of making the "wrong" decision, even the tiny one, to the point that I was a nightmare dining out. I'd have to read over the entire menu multiple times, narrow my choices down to three options, and ask the waiter which I should choose. And, honestly, I'd frequently change my choice at least once after we'd already ordered. Ridiculous, right?

Pasta vs fish dish aside, I had to learn how to make decisions without stressing and overthinking for days, or even sometimes weeks, both before and after. And you know what? I've made a lot of wrong decisions. And you know what else? I'm totally fine.

I've learned so much from every wrong choice I've made. I've learned things about myself, life, and everything in between. I've learned about running an online business; I've learned what doesn't work and what does. I used to think I made the wrong decision by waiting a few years before starting grad school. And although I was a couple of years older than most of the other counsellors-to-be in my class, if I hadn't, I may not be where I am now doing work beyond my wildest dreams. I've learned that regret doesn't serve anyone, and regardless of where I am and the choices I've made, I always get to choose how I think about them.

I'm not suggesting you intentionally make poor decisions, but do forgive yourself if you unintentionally make a "wrong" one. Do you know how hard it is to ruin your life? Much harder than your brain wants you to believe. Regretting the risotto will not lead to lasting trauma. Overthinking may be an understandable response to the uncertainties and vulnerabilities of life, but it's not helpful. Examine your thoughts, sort them out, and then drop the ones that don't serve you at the next stop. Do something. Make a mistake. You'll figure it out, keep going, and keep growing.

TAKEAWAYS

- So much of our overthinking and overanalyzing is about control. Remember the illusion of control holds us back.
- Decision-making gets caught in our attempts to control outcomes, be "right," and avoid failure. Make the best decision you can at the time and trust in your ability to cope with any outcome.
- Trust is the antidote to overanalyzing. Trust you will be able to deal with whatever happens.

Journal prompt: How would my life be different if I quieted my overthinking mind?

CHAPTER 23

SELF-SABOTAGE AND PROCRASTINATION

You want something, you start working toward it, and then, almost out of nowhere, it all falls apart. But it's not as "out of nowhere" as you may think. You actively did or didn't do something to stop yourself from getting what you wanted. At some point your brain had another thought about whether you deserved it, or once you did have it, whether you should be able to keep it, so it stopped you from getting it in the first place.

So, uh, how's it going with meeting your health goals? Have you been keeping up with your self-study courses so you can get that career upgrade? What about the menial fights you've been picking with your partner? Have you signed up for those ukulele lessons yet? Let's be honest with each other. If you have big desires, but keep putting off the work, leaving things until the last minute, distracting yourself, and committing only to inconsistency, whether you're conscious of it or not, you are self-sabotaging. You want something good but keep preventing it from happening. You procrastinate, you put it off, you avoid it, or you blow it up. Why are you doing this (especially if you had no idea this was happening)? Here are five common reasons people stop themselves from getting, or keeping, what they want:

1. *What you want is out of alignment*

   When your actions and desires are not in alignment with
   what you believe you deserve, something feels off… because
   it is. You are experiencing a lack of congruence with what
   you think you can have, and what you're doing. If you're
   not conscious of it or intentional about it, your rebel brain
   isn't going to just automatically change up those thoughts
   for you. "Yes, we can!" is not so much your brain's style.
   Instead, it will pump up all the "No, I can't" thoughts it
   possibly can. Your brain doesn't want to move forward; it
   wants to keep you right where you are.

   > I'd bet you have some pretty solid beliefs in there
   > about your worth in relation to the life you want. You
   > might often start strong and feel excited, energized,
   > and motivated to make it happen. But then, almost
   > out of nowhere, you start avoiding, procrastinating,
   > and nit-picking your way into undoing it all. Keeping
   > yourself working toward your goals will be a challenge;
   > work on those thoughts.

2. *The glass ceiling*

   Maybe you don't think you're totally undeserving of what
   you want, but you think you only deserve a certain amount.
   This one runs deep across social, political, and familial
   messaging that contributes to our beliefs about what we're
   allowed to experience. It's rough. We all have ideas about
   how high we're allowed to go before the old alignment
   alarms begin to sound and quickly bring you back to the
   level you think is more allowable for you. Unpack some of
   this in yourself. How happy are you allowed to be? How
   successful is too successful? How many accomplishments
   can you achieve before it's too much? How much is too
   much vitality? The answers are as deep as your identity and
   intertwined within it. Once you break through the ceiling,
   your beliefs about who you are and what you're allowed are
   going to make you feel terrible. If left unchecked, you'll

bring yourself back down. Don't leave them unchecked.

3. *Vulnerability avoidance*

Being vulnerable can feel terrible. It's like standing in front of a crowd, completely naked and fully exposed. Although it's just a human body—like the one every human being has—I'm willing to bet even the thought of that situation has you mentally scrambling for a T-shirt and easy-to-pull-on gym shorts. When you're vulnerable, you are exposed; you are seen for who you are. You are, quite literally, stripped down to the frame, leaving yourself open for all kinds of scrutiny.

> Trying new things, taking (reasonable) risks, going for something you want when the outcome is uncertain, allowing room for failure, and opening yourself to judgment are truly scary. The result is not in your hands and if things don't go the way you're hoping they will, it will feel terrible. Our brain's way around this is to just not do it. Even if staying where you are isn't where you want to be, your brain has convinced you it beats even the slightest chance of crashing and burning. Your brain is wrong.

4. *Imposter phenomenon*

Some days I feel like I'm on fire and others I feel like I'm burning up. A few days ago, I posted in a community of other business-owners asking if anyone else felt this way, and the answer was a resounding "YES!" It didn't matter how successful, intelligent, or educated these business-owners were. The consensus was that most people wonder if they deserve to have the love, success, authority, or leadership role they have at least some of the time. And when the doubt is strong, so is the fear of being an imposter.

> Have you ever thought, I'm not worthy of this, or, I don't deserve this, or, I must have gotten here by accident, or, It's only a matter of time before people realize that I'm a fraud? If so, then it's likely that you

have believed yourself to be an imposter. Maybe you're
experiencing it right now. These imposter thoughts
subtly creep into your mind and stop you from fully
stepping into your gifts. They try to prevent you from
moving forward because, well, it's only a matter of
time before you get found out, right? Nope. You've
got this.

5. *To protect the ego*

The fifth way you may be sabotaging yourself harkens way
back to Part Two, when we talked about avoiding failure.
Do you remember what we learned? It's just a neutral event
and, when thought of neutrally, it's merely an occurrence of
not achieving what we set out to achieve. Our ego (read: it's
your brain again) steps in and makes it mean you're inferior
or unworthy. No one really wants to feel that, so your brain
doesn't want you to bother trying. Try.

EXERCISE: MAKE IT HAPPEN

Bring to mind something you truly want in your life. It may be
a good relationship, a promotion, or the desire to feel healthy.
You may have a course you want to finish, an application you
haven't submitted yet, or a new hobby you want to try. It can
be something you've attempted previously or a dream that has
always remained out of reach. Use your journal to explore the
reasons your brain is using to stop or distract you. Then explore
the thoughts you want to intentionally foster—the thoughts that
will generate the feelings and behaviors to move you toward
your goal. Write them all down and keep them near.

Comparison

Have you ever been having a great day—maybe you've just finished a project and are enjoying the kudos, or you've achieved a personal best on the treadmill and are feeling great—and then you see on social media that someone else has done better than you? They've run faster and farther. They're at the top of their parenting, marriage, cooking skills, or company. And now you feel like crap. Comparison: one of the most common forms of self-sabotage.

Information about someone else's success bursts your bubble and deflates your beautiful feelings of accomplishment in two seconds flat. You were having a great time feeling good, but hearing about another person's accomplishment changed your whole outlook. Something (i.e., your thoughts and beliefs about what that information means) stole your sense of achievement. As usual, it's an inside job. You deflated yourself with your inner thoughts. That person was just doing their own work. No one can take away your sense of work—only you can allow that.

Comparing ourselves to others keeps us stuck, and our brain, which is trying to keep us in place, likes it that way. When was the last time you compared yourself to someone to use as a long-term motivator to make significant change in your life? Did longing after someone's fit body or successful career spur you into action to get your own? Probably not. That's not how comparison usually works, is it? All too often, when we compare ourselves to others, we use the emotional energy from that to feel terrible, and then have no fuel left to get anywhere other than the fridge… or maybe the bar.

True story: What someone else has, is, or does is simply no threat to you. What someone else has or is doesn't take away from you. Do you know the phrase, "There's enough pie for everyone"? We are all on our own journey, doing our own thing, responsible for our own lives and choices. Someone else being more put-together than you, having a more successful business than you, having a better job or marriage than you, or being a more present parent than you cannot take away from what you can create, how you can grow, what you can do. They have nothing to do with you. And truly, what someone else is doing, the success they're having, the growth they're experiencing, or the seemingly put-together life they're living is none of your business, and can only take away from your happiness if you think it can. You have no idea why someone has what they have or how they got what they've got. You don't know where they started from, how hard they worked, or how much support they had along the way. And you don't need to know. You just need to focus on you, what you want, and what you're going to do to get it.

Being run by fear

Fear is helpful when it deters you from doing something life-threatening, but not so much if it deters you from doing something important. A few summers ago, I was on a lake vacation with my family. One evening, my sister and I decided to go for a walk. And as we were walking along the quiet road lined on both sides with lush, thick forest, we looked ahead and saw three black, fuzzy objects moving in the ditch. Realizing at almost the exact same time that those balls of black fuzz were a mama black bear and her two cubs, we looked at each other and immediately turned around and walked back down the road, as if on cue. We weren't in any immediate danger, but you'd better believe my heart was pounding the entire walk back to the cabin, as I turned around every three seconds to make sure the bear family was gradually becoming three black specs in the distance.

The fear we both felt in that moment was extremely useful. It prompted our quick decision to turn around and escape the dangerous situation immediately. Unfortunately, most of our fear instinct isn't being used to prevent us from dying; it's keeping us from living. We use fear to stop ourselves from existing in the ways that may just be the most important. Speaking up is not dangerous. Starting your dream business is not dangerous. Going for a promotion is not dangerous. Vulnerable conversations are not dangerous. Saying "no" is not dangerous. Being yourself, with or without the approval of others, is not dangerous.

What have you let fear talk you out of in your life? Going back to school to earn that diploma because it's too late to start a new career? Starting that business because your friends will think it's stupid? Asking that person out because they may say no? Saying "I love you" because they might not reciprocate? Sharing your idea because Dave from accounting may say it's dumb? Telling Uncle Jim racist comments are not welcome in your home in case he gets embarrassed?

Ask yourself—are any of these real threats? To my ego, maybe. To my life? No. You are the conscious being in charge of your own choices; fear does not deserve the privilege of stopping you. Yes, fear may come along for the ride, but fear doesn't get to drive. It's okay to do things with fear. It's okay to try scared—that may be the only way you can do it.

It's not brave to do easy things. You don't have to be brave to get a glass of water unless you have burning-hot coals covering your living-room floor between you and the faucet. To be brave takes a level of risk. Otherwise, you're just doing something regular. And if you're always doing regular things, you're probably missing the richer and more fulfilling human experiences that are available to you.

Much of what you have is a result of how you've been participating in your life (or not). To get results, you must take action. The actions you take will create your results. And your behavior is determined by your feelings. And your feelings are generated by your thoughts.

I'm not going to sit here from my place of white, Canadian, educated, middle-class privilege and claim you always have control over your circumstances. I will say, however, that you always have choices within them. And to choose different, you have to feel different. In order to feel different, you have to think different.

And remember: Your thoughts are always up to you.

TAKEAWAYS

- Raising your self-worth immediately neutralizes many of your self-sabotaging behaviors. If you believe you deserve a better life, you will be able to take the steps to get there.
- Comparison is within our control; it's something we do to ourselves. Life is not a zero-sum game. Someone's success does not take away our own unless we let it.
- Our self-sabotaging behaviors are rooted in our self-worth and desire to protect ourselves from uncomfortable emotions and thoughts. We need to get strong and trust in our ability to aim high and cope with any potential consequences.

Journal prompt: Where do I see self-sabotage coming up most in my life? What can I do to turn it around?

ARE YOU READY TO DRIVE YOUR OWN DARN BUS?

Remember Heather's thoughts and feelings about her mom's propensity for comments about her parenting? Remember when I freaked out that my friend's lack of response meant I wasn't lovable, so I made myself feel even more alone? Remember how many emotions can arrive based only on how you look at any given situation? Remember the ABCBO model?

Now you can clearly see the interconnectedness of your emotions, thoughts, behaviors, and outcomes. If you want a different outcome, pick a different behavior; if you want to take a different action, you need to feel differently; and if you want to feel differently, you have to take the driver's seat and take your brain to a different thought.

After deep-diving into so many of the emotions, thoughts, and behaviors humans experience without really understanding why, now you get to see that a whole new world of self-understanding has been opened up for you. Maybe you're feeling liberated. Maybe your perfectionist brain is telling you to figure it out before you can try it. Maybe you need time to reflect and digest.

There is one thing I want you to keep in mind since you have invested in yourself page after page: don't do this work to become a better person. You don't need to. You're not a person who needs to be "better." You're a person with ups and downs and strengths and areas to grow, just like everyone else. This work is not about becoming better; it's about feeling better and living better not because you need to, but because you want to. If you want to integrate and assimilate what you've learned in this book—great! You'll feel better, like others better, like yourself better, and enjoy your short time on this planet more. If you don't want to—also great! You don't have to. You're allowed to not feel better, and it doesn't make you any worse or any less of a person. If you decide to take this work seriously and implement even half of what you learned in this book, you will unmess your mind and change your life.

Someone asked me once how they would know when they were driving their own darn bus, so I want to make sure you look out for signs that you're on the right road.

First, you are able to respond instead of react to previously triggering situations, conversations, and interactions. When something upsets you or triggers an emotional response, you are able to take a few seconds, step back, take a breath, evaluate, and get curious about your thoughts, and ultimately understand the stories you are telling yourself. And only when you're more clear about it will you respond in a mature, responsible, and respectful way. It means you're using the STOPP process, and it's a game-changer.

Second, you allow other people to not like you, not approve of you, and not agree with you. You don't try to make people be okay with you because you are okay with who you are. One of the reasons we think we need *others* to be happy with who we are is because we think this means *we* can be okay with who we are. But if you're doing your work to value yourself, then you won't need positive opinions and approval in order to be okay with yourself. You also don't need a perfect house/

job/partner or social calendar to tell you that. You don't need to people-please or pretend to be someone else.

Third, you know that nothing is personal. It's a good sign you're moving forward when you understand people are not doing things against you; they are doing things for themselves. You know other people are not making you miserable or out to get you. You know most of your difficult feelings are being created by your own thoughts.

Fourth, you know when to recognize that you're being unkind to yourself. It's a huge sign of progress when you're able to stop the self-criticisms about to overcome you, and pay attention to what your inner monologue is saying. You see clearly when your mind is spinning out of control with ways your failure is a part of your identity, and are able to trade those nasty words for some that are kinder.

Fifth, you recognize fear for what it is and can see more clearly what your primitive brain is doing. You get a stressful email and feel your breathing start to quicken, your heart is racing, and your hands are clammy. You notice this and quickly remind yourself that your negativity bias is treating this situation like a threat to your life. You know it is not, so you take a break and remember that you are the driver of your own darn bus, and you won't go down the road to Self-Unraveling Town.

So much of what you have in your life has been created by your own choices, and now you know what it takes to change. So, call out the BS in your brain when it tries to avoid difficult emotions and take the easy path. But also go easy on yourself. Be patient.

As you do the work, I can't overstate the importance of self-care and self-compassion. I know how I value myself and how I feel is not contingent on what other people think about me; it's grounded in what *I* think about me. And I want you to do the same. Acknowledge how far you've come instead of thinking that you have so far to go. Be proud of yourself. Recognize the steps you've taken, the shifts you've made, and the growing you've done. You can't always see your growth every single day, but if you check in with the you now versus the you a few short weeks or months ago, you'll see it. The human brain likes to look forward, anticipate pitfalls, and worry about what's coming. It's your job to direct your own big grey mass to look in the rearview mirror to see where you were, appreciate where you are now, and be excited about where else you're going.

Pay attention to your true self—the self under all the pleasing, perfecting, performing, proving, justifying, and defending. The self who feels free to think, feel, and be whomever he, she, or they want to be. Observe them. Be intentional with them. Connect with them. Listen to them. Ignore your carful of critics who attempt to throw you off-course. They don't get to make your decisions for you.

We all want someone to tell us there's another way, an easier way—a way in which we can sit on the couch and binge Netflix while our lives and relationships and goals and dreams just work themselves out. If I could show you that way of doing things, I would. If there was an easy way around the work, trust me, I'd tell you. Until the easy way is discovered, know I'm in the trenches with you every day working on my true self without apology so I can think and feel with authenticity, while I continue to create the intentional life I want.

We're going to work together as we step into our power to reprogram our thinking and shift our reality. We will take on our primitive brain and its drive to hold us back and keep us comfortable in our discomfort. We will not shy away from taking on our old, learned, unhelpful, and unhealthy thought patterns or habitual behaviors. We will create what we want for ourselves, our lives, our relationships, our goals, and our dreams. We are brave, honest, and vulnerable. We will do the work. Because when you do the work to create the life you want, you can stand back and be proud of the work you've done and how far you've come. And believe me, you've come far.

Everything can be taken from a man but one thing: the last of the human freedoms—to choose one's attitude in any given set of circumstances, to choose one's own way.

—Viktor Frankl, Holocaust survivor

WATKINS

Sharing Wisdom Since 1893

The story of Watkins began in 1893, when scholar of esotericism John Watkins founded our bookshop, inspired by the lament of his friend and teacher Madame Blavatsky that there was nowhere in London to buy books on mysticism, occultism or metaphysics. That moment marked the birth of Watkins, soon to become the publisher of many of the leading lights of spiritual literature, including Carl Jung, Rudolf Steiner, Alice Bailey and Chögyam Trungpa.

Today, the passion at Watkins Publishing for vigorous questioning is still resolute. Our stimulating and groundbreaking list ranges from ancient traditions and complementary medicine to the latest ideas about personal development, holistic wellbeing and consciousness exploration. We remain at the cutting edge, committed to publishing books that change lives.

DISCOVER MORE AT:
www.watkinspublishing.com

Read our blog

Watch and listen to
our authors in action

Sign up to
our mailing list

We celebrate conscious, passionate, wise and happy living.
Be part of that community by visiting

 /watkinspublishing   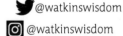 @watkinswisdom

/watkinsbooks   @watkinswisdom